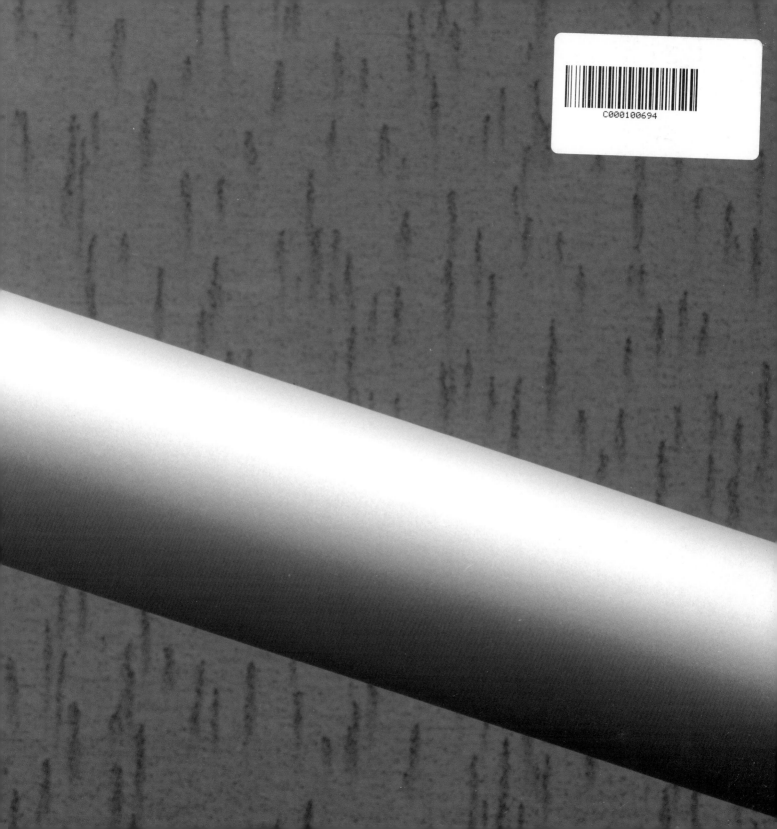

BALTIC: THE ART FACTORY

BALTIC

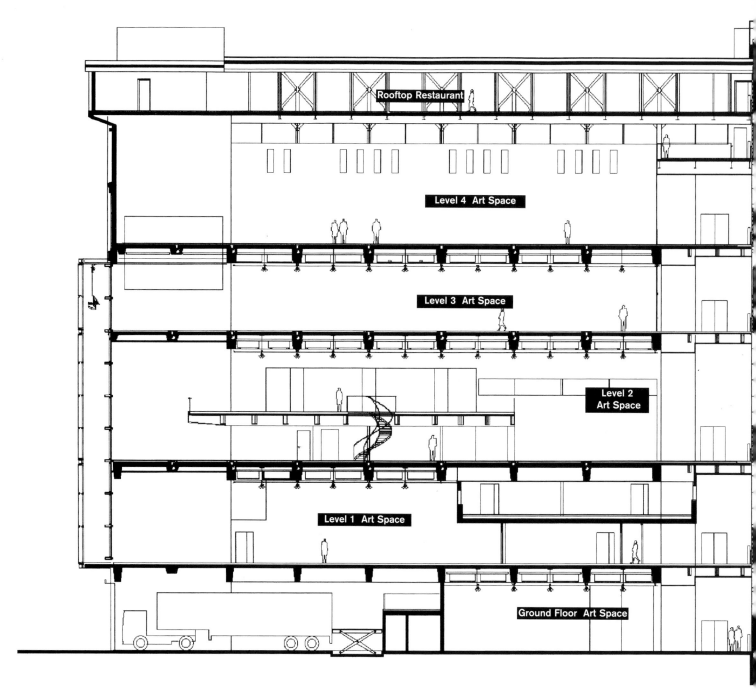

Rooftop Restaurant

Level 4 Art Space

Level 3 Art Space

Level 2
Art Space

Level 1 Art Space

Ground Floor Art Space

MAIN BUILDING

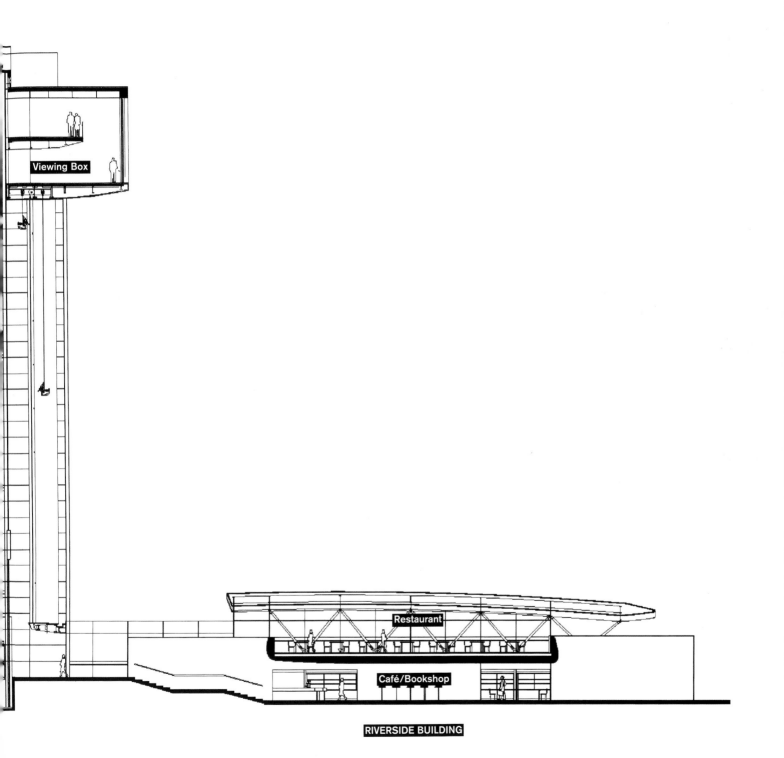

Viewing Box

Restaurant

Café/Bookshop

RIVERSIDE BUILDING

Contents

Foreword

At the start of the 21st century there is a recognised need for a 'third place', a place which is neither work nor home, where people can engage in a stimulating intellectual environment and where the edges between learning and leisure, education and entertainment, are blurred, where people are excited and have fun, even although they may, on occasion, be challenged.

BALTIC provides that place, that intellectual pantheon, where people will gravitate to before or after work, simply to be there. BALTIC will bring a new dimension to people's perception of the visual arts and also to the complex relationship between art and education. It is about what you will experience by feel, by touch, and by pressure upon your every emotion.

But BALTIC is not just about art. BALTIC will be a place where people can come simply to hang out in the café, in the Riverside Restaurant or in the Rooftop Restaurant, to browse through the bookshop, or simply to sit in Baltic Square enjoying one of the most amazing views in the world. As Chairman, I am extremely excited about the way in which it will be an exemplary Pan-European demonstration of how people can connect at all sorts of levels with the visual arts, and equally importantly, how cultural projects can accelerate urban renaissance. BALTIC has been, and will continue to be, a catalyst for the regeneration of Gateshead Quays and a strong affirmation of the cultural square mile straddling the Tyne.

Interest in and recognition of the work being undertaken at BALTIC was clearly brought home to me in 1999, over three years before the opening, when I visited the Miró Foundation in Barcelona. The first image to greet me on my arrival was the BALTIC Newsletter on the notice board, a significant endorsement by one of Europe's pre-eminent art institutions of what was to happen in Gateshead at some time in the future. This level of interest has been sustained throughout the world and ensures BALTIC a place on the international art map.

I am certain that BALTIC will bring to the British art scene a new dimension in the visual arts. Uniquely it will have no collection, but instead a series of galleries and studios featuring high quality, fresh, innovative work, much of it by artists of international acclaim, and nearly all commissioned for, or even made in, BALTIC itself. BALTIC will create new audiences and push the boundaries of contemporary art, providing artists and audiences with opportunities to create original and experimental work using traditional and new media. The artistic programme will be one of the most adventurous and polemic undertaken in the UK, and I am looking forward to sharing and enjoying it with the hundreds of thousands of people who will visit BALTIC in the years ahead.

Alan J. Smith
Chairman

From Flour Mill to Art Factory: a preface

'Our objective in the development and conversion of the Baltic Flour Mills is to provide a national and international centre for contemporary visual arts with large, temporary exhibition spaces. Both in scale and artistic policy it would be unique in this country and one of only half a dozen comparable facilities in the world.'

These are the first two sentences of Gateshead Council's ambitious brief for the architectural competition of April 1994. Eight years later, as BALTIC opens its doors to the public for the first time, this is exactly what has been achieved. Over the years, many people have been involved in making this happen, but never has the fundamental ambition been questioned or compromised. First of all, to make it a possibility and to convince others to support the project, a specific place was needed that could meet these high expectations. The silo building of the old mill was not the first, or even the most obvious of the different options – it was definitely not the easiest of buildings to convert – but finally, it turned out to be the perfect choice.

'Contemporary visual artists require large spaces for their works to be seen at their best and this fact is reflected internationally in buildings and building conversions which provide exhibitions and related exhibition work to develop and extend the appreciation of the work of living artists.'

Reading the competition brief from 1994 reveals that there was a strong desire that the Baltic Flour Mills – which at that time was still the name of both the building itself and the future project – should also be a regional venue that responded to the immediate needs of the arts in the North East. The ambition was to have at least a part of the building finished just two years later, for the 1996 Year of Visual Arts, and to be able to host the tour of the 1995 British Art Show.

This turned out to be an impossible timescale. However, to 'do it all' has been the ambition of BALTIC since the very start, and one that finally, we have been able to meet. Since the summer of 1997, when the funding was in place, it has been a matter of being sufficiently sensitive to the place in which this new institution is located and to understand the context in which it will be working: its potential freedom as well as its inherited responsibilities.

BALTIC will be global and local at the same time. It will provide the same cutting-edge facilities and generous opportunities for regional, national and international art and artists in a balanced, accessible and exciting programme. But in order to be truly an Art Factory, and in addition to displaying the art of our time and working creatively with artists to realise projects, the focus must be on the *process* of making art as much as on the final product. BALTIC will invite a range of creative people to take part in its generous residency programme to ensure that the whole region, not just the institution, benefits from their stay: keeping the brick walls of BALTIC as transparent and open as possible.

Anish Kapoor's installation *TARATANTARA* during the summer of 1999 was the definitive division between the building's industrial past and its creative future: a fanfare heralding the new life of this former flour mill as a centre for contemporary art.

In spite of its name, BALTIC is in the North East of England. The old mill may have got its name from this region's historical connections with Scandinavia, from the Viking invasions a millennium ago or from today's ferry routes to Norway, Denmark and Sweden. It could also have come from Joseph Rank – who named all the mills he founded around the country after different seas and oceans – although there is no mention of this in his biography (R.G. Burnett, *Through the Mill: The Life of Joseph Rank*, 1945). However, the title page of this book carries the motto *'Man shall not live by bread alone'.* So true: we also need art and spectacle. This is what BALTIC will offer: the necessities that both sustain and enrich all our lives.

The BALTIC building has five art spaces to accommodate any kind of art – including a 'museum level', in which temperature and humidity can be controlled to meet the requirements of more sensitive works – as well as spaces for any form of contemporary creation: studios, workshops and media labs. Throughout the long history of this project, and the differing views of the many people who have contributed to it over the years, architect Dominic Williams' design has stood the test of time. Its fundamental idea is one of simplicity, honesty and flexibility, in both materials as well as use of spaces. Having had the good fortune to work with him in the final stages of the design process in 1997–98,

I was able to add my own experience of running both a temporary exhibition venue and an artist residency programme to his scheme. The result is an interior design that subtly and sensitively reflects the industrial heritage of this building, whilst simultaneously and unashamedly creating something new.

The walk around BALTIC with the architect, contained in this book, provides a personal picture of the building before it was finished and ready to be opened to the public. Similarly, John Riddy's stunning photographs, taken in June 2002, capture the building as it looked just one month before the opening. The time line section at the back of this book tells the history of the project, not as a narrative story, but in a series of 'flashes' that highlight the important steps on the long road to BALTIC. It also includes other key moments in the creative history of the region, in order to provide a context for the development of BALTIC.

This is the old Baltic Flour Mill, busy for thirty years as a site for the production of flour; derelict for nearly twenty years and now, after another five, suddenly accessible to everyone as a place to meet artists and their work. Entering the former grain silo – free of charge – is to enter a familiar, yet unknown building: like a magic house in your own backyard, a Wonderland on safe territory. And one in which you are more prepared to meet the challenge posed by the art of our time. Contemporary artists work with contemporary matters; matters that can be both difficult and disturbing but which artists can reveal to us anew as spectacular, amazing and beautiful.

When Jaume Plensa's light beam *Blake in Gateshead* is lit again on the night of 13 July, everyone who sees it will know: this is where it is. This is where it is going to happen!

Welcome.

Sune Nordgren
Director

A Walk Through

BALTIC

On 10 January 2002

Preamble

When Sune Nordgren, Dominic Williams and myself first talked about this book, we were all in agreement that we wanted to steer away from the traditional academic essay. We were keen that the text should be the outcome of discussions concerning the ideas and processes behind the design of BALTIC. Coming from an architectural design background myself, I am particularly interested in the notion of site-specific writing: writing that emerges out of an engagement with site. In the case of BALTIC, the site is not only a material reality – the architecture of the built form – but it is also a cultural entity: the team of people involved in generating the concept of BALTIC and making it manifest.

I believe that we can best understand buildings, the ways in which they have developed and their past, present and future occupations, by moving through them. A strong relationship evolves between inner reflection and outer reality, between knowing and walking, as we experience a journey through a space. For this reason, this text is a record of a conversation that took place during a walk around BALTIC on 10 January 2002. Three voices are 'visibly' present: Dominic Williams of Ellis Williams Architects, architect of BALTIC; Sune Nordgren, Director of BALTIC, and my own. However, there are many other voices that have greatly influenced the shape of this walk, both through words and through actions, especially Sarah Martin, Assistant Curator, BALTIC; Emma Thomas, Education and Public Programme Manager, BALTIC and Jason Geen, architect on site for Ellis Willliams Architects.

This text is envisioned as a kind of tour that will take you around the building and in so doing, unravel the history of the making of BALTIC. The walk engages both with the previous use of BALTIC as a flour mill and the more recent process of creating a space for contemporary artists, art and audiences. We will pause at various points to focus on specific spaces, objects and events with the intention that BALTIC is understood as an evolving and shared event. The artworks, galleries and architectural sites discussed here are given full references at the end of the book. Likewise, those exhibitions and events in BALTIC's pre-opening programme, B4B, referred to during the conversation are included, in more detail, in the time line section of this book.

Jane Rendell
Lecturer in Architecture, The Bartlett School of Architecture, University College, London

The Entrance:
'it's very much like entering a ferry!'

Sune Nordgren: BALTIC has quite a low entrance. It's dark, because of the Cor-Ten steel. To me, it's very much like entering a ferry! You squeeze into the ferry and then it opens up and you're out on the sea. It's similar here: you come in and the 'entrance street' is quite low. But then there's an enormous light that draws you into the building.

Dominic Williams: That's right. Even though the position of the entrance has moved around a lot during the design of BALTIC, looking up has always been an important part of arriving here. The Riverside Building does a crucial job in providing an easy step up from Baltic Square.

Jane Rendell: Crossing the Millennium Bridge (designed by Wilkinson Eyre Architects and Gifford & Partners) will be many people's first approach to BALTIC. The bridge is an optimistic symbol, but not simply one of connection. The German cultural critic Georg Simmel has suggested that the reason bridges are such strong symbols, is that they both separate and connect. I like this notion because it allows both sides to be connected whilst retaining their own identities, which is important for the relationship between Gateshead and Newcastle.

Cor-Ten Steel:
'it's about the feel of the material itself'

Jane Rendell: The strategic use of materials strikes me as absolutely essential to the concept of BALTIC. It helps position people in relation to the building's past and its new use.

Dominic Williams: Sune and I have talked about materials a lot; about how you combine old and new. Should new match old? Not a very honest approach! We were looking for a material that crossed old and new somehow, and that also connected BALTIC to its context. Cor-Ten steel interested me. I used to walk past John Winter's house in Highgate, London, and we also went to see the Cummins Factory near Doncaster: pieces of architecture that use Cor-Ten in different ways. Cor-Ten develops a naturalised, oxidised coating on its surface which makes it very good as a cladding material. It has been used for a long time in this area for building bridges and ships. Antony Gormley also used Cor-Ten for the *Angel of the North* in Gateshead.

Jane Rendell: The building looks old but it's interesting to note that the Baltic Flour Mills weren't built until 1950, although the foundation work began in the late 1930s and was halted by the onset of the war. From 1858 this site was occupied by an iron and steel works famous for constructing the High Level Bridge. The Cor-Ten steel makes links to the history of this site and its context without being nostalgic, and also creates a visual connection between BALTIC's old silo building and the new Riverside Building.

Dominic Williams: Yes, Cor-Ten is used to finish the towers of the old flour mill building and in the new Riverside Building.

Jane Rendell: Have you been deliberate in creating a palette of materials?

Dominic Williams: Yes. For example, we wanted to introduce a material different to Cor-Ten, so we brought in aluminium on all the new structures we created, such as the viewing box. Cor-Ten is a rusty, old material, and aluminium is a newer, car-like material, hinting at the new currencies happening within the building.

Sune Nordgren: If you compare BALTIC with other new buildings, we have used relatively few materials.

Jane Rendell: The palette is simple but rich and the materials you have chosen for BALTIC are all about tactility and juxtaposition.

Dominic Williams: Cor-Ten is quite monolithic when you look at it from a distance, but it is a material where close-up, you can see lots more detail.

Sune Nordgren: We tried to get away from painting and covering. So as far as possible it's about the feel of the material itself. But it's also about materials that are, in many ways, natural.

Dominic Williams: The slate we have used on the ground floor and on the back wall of the café comes from the ground: a real, earth-like material. The materials are very honest, very straightforward.

Jane Rendell: The selection and use of materials is very modernist in that respect: truth to materials, form reflecting function, and so on. But there is also a concern with extending the natural into the cultural, bringing natural elements into the building. The design has aspects of the minimal in its approach, not minimalist in an architectural 'look at the cleverness of this simple detail' sort of way, but more in line with minimalism in art, and the concern with perception and the experience of the viewer.

The Bookshop: 'think time'

Jane Rendell: Cafés and bookshops have become increasingly important in the design of new spaces for art, especially ones that don't charge an entrance fee. At times this can reinforce the desire to make places like galleries and museums more accessible. Would you say this is the case at BALTIC?

Sune Nordgren: It's free to get into BALTIC. We like that, of course. But we need to get income and we want to encourage people to stay. Lots of the artists we will be working with are not household names in this region or, indeed, in Britain. So we have to attract people to BALTIC as a place in itself. With some contemporary art you don't necessarily like it immediately: you have to go back, or take part in a workshop or a guided tour, or read a little bit more about it. If admission is free you can stay longer, have a coffee and so on. It's important that the retail area and the bookshop are an extension of the programme; a reflection of the building and of BALTIC as a whole.

Jane Rendell: Graphics and the use of typography have been a strong element in creating an identity for BALTIC. You've published a lot of material already: the BALTIC Newsletter and books such as the B.READ series. Is this an important part of your history as a publisher, Sune?

Sune Nordgren: Yes, of course. For me, apart from my discussions with Dominic, the BALTIC typeface was the start of the whole process. The printed material we send out has to reflect the project as well as give information about it. BALTIC was an old industrial building: rough, black and white, simple. So that's the basis of the choice for the graphic identity, which is based on an old woodblock typeface from the 1940s.

Jane Rendell: The design of the bookshop suggests it is a place where you would like people to browse and sit down to read the material.

Sune Nordgren: Exactly. The layout of the bookshop is in three stages: you enter it and have the catalogues, postcards, posters and perhaps some souvenirs. Further in, you have the art reference books, the art magazines. Then further in again are the more expensive books, where you might want to sit down and have a look before you buy something.

Dominic Williams: When we were looking at places where people could read books or browse, we thought about having views out of the windows for people to think. 'Think time' is really important. So the windows in the bookshop give glimpses out to the Quayside and bridge. They act as a balance: you can lose yourself in books or you can sit and look out.

Jane Rendell: I often get a sense of panic in bookshops: 'how will I ever get through all this material?' So for me the windows provide a chance to 'look up and out'; not really think time, more time *not* to think, to be able to look beyond and get a brief escape! But they also provide carefully framed views that link you back to the outside world.

abcdefghijklmnopq
rstuvwxyzåäö
ABCDEFGHIJKLMNO
PQRSTUVWXYZÅÄÖ
1234567890 @.,'""
"":;-–+ =)(/%£$&!?

B. BALTIC

The Café:
'we wanted the kind of simplicity the slate has'

Jane Rendell: The slate is a strong design feature in the café. Where does it come from?

Dominic Williams: We made several trips to Blaenau Ffestiniog in Wales to look at slate. For the ground floor we used a standard roofing module, which is easily replaceable, to create a 'total surface'. Along the back wall of the café, against South Shore Road, we used 30mm strips of riven-faced slate to build up the retaining wall. It was important to bring in some detail, to be able to read the edges of a real material.

Sune Nordgren: The mortar is pulled back so it looks like a dry-stone wall. It really looks like these walls that you see everywhere in Wales.

Dominic Williams: Yes, the slate looks like it's just been stacked up.

Sune Nordgren: We also wanted the kind of simplicity that slate has on our ground floor. You can see these slate floors in old barns and so on.

Dominic Williams: It's so simply cut: they hit the top of the slate and it falls apart into thinner leaves.

Jane Rendell: You talk of the slate as a natural material, but what about the effects of quarrying on the landscape?

Dominic Williams: The use of any material involves some sort of environmental consideration, and we have been aware all along of choosing environmentally-aware solutions. The quarry had already started a scheme for grassing over the original quarry. In Wales, it's about employment as well.

Jaume Plensa, 'Blake in Gateshead' (1996): 'the world needs artists' eyes'

Jane Rendell: Integral to the making of BALTIC has been the making of art, right from the start. Just off the Riverside Walk is the light sculpture *Blake in Gateshead*, by Jaume Plensa.

Sune Nordgren: The light beam was first installed just outside the main building, in the middle of what's now the Riverside Building. It was originally commissioned by Gateshead Council for the Visual Arts Year in 1996, as part of the 'Temporary Contemporary', which was a series of commissions on and around the Baltic Flour Mills to focus attention on the building before the Lottery bid was made. It was a very strong, positive statement that something was going to happen. The quotation from Blake around the base of the sculpture reads '*No Bird Soars too High if he Soars with his own Wings*'. It comes from 'The Proverbs of Hell' in *The Marriage of Heaven and Hell*. It's a good motto for an organisation that will fly high – and always with its own wings – which is partly why we decided to re-install it permanently outside BALTIC. It will be lit for exhibition openings and other special events as a kind of signal. It's also a bit like coming full-circle: many people will remember the piece from '96, so it seemed to make sense to light it again once BALTIC opens.

Dominic Williams: The Plensa sculpture is interesting to me because it is about the visual distortion of space. If you look at it one way you see a very straight beam going up, but if you look at it from another angle, it appears to bend, even cross the river. This aspect of distortion has always been a theme of the building, which changed in size and shape every time we looked at it. Artists who have worked with this building, such as Plensa and also Anish Kapoor, have thought about space in this way.

Jane Rendell: The decision to work with artists throughout the process of designing a building for art is quite popular at present. You only have to think of the Ikon in Birmingham, where the artist Tania Kovats worked with architects Levitt Bernstein, or at the New Art Gallery in Walsall, where artists Richard Wentworth and Catherine Yass among others, worked with architects Caruso St. John. And then there is the on-going c/PLEX Project in West Bromwich, where Alsop Architects have been working with Jubilee Arts and various artists to create a new centre for artistic innovation in community arts practice.

Sune Nordgren: The pre-opening arts programme, B4B, which has been running since 1998, has worked in parallel with the building development and involved a wide range of approaches to working with artists and artworks. For example, there have been site-specific works, such as Anish Kapoor's *TARATANTARA* (1999) and historical exhibitions, like 'Kurt Schwitters' at the Hatton Gallery (1999). Then there have been commissions and co-commissions in non-art venues, such as Marijke Van Warmerdam's *Weather Forecast* (2001) and the sound installation *Forty Part Motet* by Janet Cardiff, shown at the Castle Keep in Newcastle in 2001 and now in Tate's collection. We also brought in Julian Opie as a kind of artistic reference. He worked closely with the design team very early on.

Dominic Williams: There were strategic points within the design process at which things happened. I think the biggest leap that was taken was with Anish Kapoor's installation, *TARATANTARA*. We used the pause between two different building contracts to do that.

Sune Nordgren: It took a lot of effort and money, but it was worth every penny, because it was such a symbolic thing. It was the absolute division between the past and the future of the building. BALTIC was almost nothing at that time: it was just a hollow void that held the sculpture. It brought life back to a building that had been derelict for about twenty years.

Dominic Williams: Yes, and it brought people into the building again.

Jane Rendell: Having only seen the video documentary about the installation of the sculpture, I understand the work more as an event that marked a moment in time. It seemed to make a ritual of the new inhabitation.

Sune Nordgren: At the time, BALTIC was a building site: quite dirty and busy and it was difficult to get over the Tyne Bridge and down to the building. But lots of people made an effort – 16,000 visitors in eight weeks – which showed that there was a lot of potential interest.

Jane Rendell: The strongest thing for me that comes out of the work itself concerns the transition between inside and outside. It was the first and the only time that I have seen the inside of the building with the silos removed. *TARATANTARA* worked to bring the inside out and the outside in.

Sune Nordgren: Exactly. Normally with Anish's work you look inside it. But in this case he revealed the whole thing. From outside the building you looked inside the sculpture: very typical Anish Kapoor. But then from inside the building, you saw the outside of the sculpture.

Dominic Williams: It was fantastic to be able to see both the whole volume of the building for the first time, and to see how this piece distorted that volume.

Jane Rendell: It's interesting though because that particular exposure of the inside, without the silos, will never be seen again. Did this experience influence the process of design?

Sune Nordgren: The Kapoor piece was inspirational for Dominic, and for all of us, because it was so very much about art and architecture in symbiosis.

Jane Rendell: Many artists seem increasingly interested in architecture and space, and tend to see buildings in a different way. It is easy to get bogged down in all the detailing, economics and legalities of architecture, so having a different perspective is important.

Dominic Williams: I think it's important that architects should be able to work with artists on any project. Architects always have many dominant pressures from other parties – first the usability, then the money, and also politics – so it's interesting to have artists' views. They look at all these things totally differently. The world needs artists' eyes.

Jane Rendell: I think this is quite useful for architecture, not just from a visual perspective, but keeping hold of a critical viewpoint is important. Although artists might not have always worked with the building itself or influenced the programme, you have had artists like Jenny Holzer using the building as a backdrop for projecting her work, and photographers documenting the making of BALTIC, like Etienne Clément. This process of photographic documentation has been something that a number of new art spaces have adopted. For example, Catherine Yass photographed the building process at Tate Modern.

From Flour Mill to Art Factory:
'Tate Modern of the North?'

Jane Rendell: When you look up at the old silo building, from down here in the Riverside Building, you realise just what an impact this structure has in terms of mass and volume: the building stored 22,000 tons of wheat in 148 concrete silos.

Dominic Williams: Yes, when you say, 'We've been working on BALTIC,' people say, 'Oh, that building. I remember that building.' It's ingrained, people remember it.

Sune Nordgren: We are in a familiar building which is a strength since, in many ways, we come from outside. I'm a stranger, BALTIC is a stranger; most of the things we will be working with are unfamiliar: it's contemporary art, it's challenging and new. So there is definitely an advantage to being in a building that is familiar. People are curious because they've seen the reconstruction over the past four years. They want to get in and see what it's all about. When we open, people will be going back to BALTIC. Even though some of them will never have been inside, they will still be going back to something that is familiar.

Jane Rendell: The *Baltic Memories* project has been interesting in this respect. The documentary film you commissioned from A19 Film and Video delves into a huge amount of archival material. It's important to remember that the silo building, where the wheat was stored, is the only remaining part of a larger factory complex for making and storing flour and animal feed. Other parts of the mill were destroyed by fire in 1976. In the film, people such as the silo foreman, who kept records for each storage bin, the sack workers, who blew air into the sacks to clean them, and the laboratory and bakery staff who tested the grain, describe in detail what happened in each bit of the building.

Sune Nordgren: *Baltic Memories* was one of the first B4B projects, made with Gateshead Council Arts and Libraries Department, the Shipley Art Gallery in Gateshead and Tyne and Wear Museums in 1998–99. It was important for us to get feedback on the history of the building from the people who actually used to work there.

Jane Rendell: What comes out of *Baltic Memories* is the building as a place of production, a factory, with the silos as a place for the storage of wheat and the mills as places for the making of flour and animal feed. But the building complex was also part of a much larger system of distribution, a point of destination for wheat coming in by ship from Canada, Russia, Australia, India, France and Argentina, and a point of departure for flour going out by tanker lorry to bakers and retailers worldwide.

Sune Nordgren: It's nice to be able to say that BALTIC is a development from a flour mill to an Art Factory.

Jane Rendell: What exactly is an 'Art Factory'? In trying to understand what BALTIC will be like when it is up and running, it's good to compare it with existing models.

Sune Nordgren: Yes, I don't mind if people say, for example, 'This is the Tate Modern of the North,' because it puts them on the right track. Then you can tell them what the differences are. The primary difference, of course, is that BALTIC will not have a permanent collection like Tate. It is a place where the art of our time is produced and exhibited: an Art Factory rather than a museum.

Jane Rendell: What about P.S.1 in Queens, New York: an art space in an old school building, that aims to integrate the production and the showing of art?

Sune Nordgren: Yes, P.S.1 is a bit like us, a place where artists can go and work. But it's more of a museum than BALTIC will be.

Dominic Williams: You could probably relate BALTIC to the European Kunsthalle idea [*Kunsthalle,* from the German, literally 'art hall'] of a purpose-built space for temporary exhibitions. It is about getting away from the static museum and moving towards something that is perhaps less controlled and more about change.

Sune Nordgren: Dominic came to my previous place, Malmö Konsthall in Sweden, pretty early on and saw this very simple purpose-built building: it looks like an enormous artist's studio.

Dominic Williams: It could have housed cars, a garage almost.

Sune Nordgren: The simplicity and flexibility of BALTIC is based on my experience of running both a contemporary art space and an artist-in-residence programme [IASPIS, International Artist Studio Program in Sweden] from 1996 to 1998. And also, of course, on the opportunities that Dominic's design opened up.

Dominic Williams: My initial concept was always the four main floors and the Rooftop Restaurant, and that was it. It hasn't changed at all from that.

Sune Nordgren: The Art Factory idea is not only based on the fact that BALTIC is an old building, but also on the fact that we are based in Gateshead. We will need to invite creative people to come to us and use the unique facilities we can offer. Even if it is an old industrial building on the outside, on the inside it will be very new and cutting-edge in its technology.

Jane Rendell: So in a way it is very different from the old building, where each part of the architecture was designed to house a specific process. With BALTIC, the concept of the factory is still about production, but this time the design is about flexibility rather than specificity.

Dominic Williams: Which makes it easy in one sense because there is no brief. But without a collection it's very difficult to anticipate or predict what will happen in the building. How do you design for artworks that might be made or shown in the future without knowing the context?

Jane Rendell: In this respect it reminds me a little of the Wapping Project in London. Wapping also has no permanent collection. I've been having similar discussions with Jules Wright, the curator, about the excitement, but also the difficulties, of designing for potential. Wapping is also an old industrial building whose past use greatly influenced the initial layout and details of the design. But it is different from BALTIC in terms of size – it is much smaller, and the attitude to commissioning has a site-specific focus. What is your attitude to commissioning site-specific work at BALTIC?

Sune Nordgren: We haven't commissioned any permanent, site-specific work for the building. Artists have, of course, responded both to the building and to the region through commissions.

For example, Chris Burden is constructing a scale model, in Meccano, of the Tyne Bridge for the opening in July. I see BALTIC very much as a container. BALTIC should keep its low-key flexibility and openness so that anything can happen in this building. Apart from Jaume Plensa's light beam, it's all on a temporary basis.

Jane Rendell: The pre-opening programme has connected BALTIC with other local sites. But what about working with other art commissioning agencies that are already located in the area itself?

Sune Nordgren: Well, they are here and so are we, so there will be opportunities to collaborate. There are already a number of artists' initiatives in Newcastle, like Locus+ and Waygood Gallery. We also have six universities and a number of art colleges in the region, as well as museums like the Laing Art Gallery in Newcastle and the Shipley Art Gallery in Gateshead, both part of Tyne and Wear Museums. We have started to work with these existing institutions through our pre-opening programme, which has been running for almost four years now. It has been very important for us to show ourselves as a partner in the region, as well as signalling the kinds of things we would like to do in the future. So we have already collaborated with galleries and individuals – and we will continue to do this of course – but BALTIC itself will also generate activities of various kinds. If we want to strengthen the arts scene in the North East, we need to bring people to the region and encourage them to stay for a while. That's also one of the reasons why, very early on, we set up the BALTIC Chair in Contemporary Art at the University of Newcastle [currently held, until 2003, by artist Susan Hiller], as well as the artist-in-residence programme.

The Silos:
'strangers in their own land'

Jane Rendell: BALTIC, the silo house, is the only one left of a complex of five buildings. The other buildings were destroyed by fire, but the silo house proved too expensive to demolish and survived. One of the most contentious things for me about the design was the early decision not to keep any of the silos, even as a reminder, given their unique qualities and history. This is something that might puzzle people. Perhaps you could say something about the decisions made to remove them?

Dominic Williams: We thought about all these issues very carefully. Keeping the silos would have been very restrictive. When we originally looked at it, we had ideas where we retained some of the silos, chiselled out spaces and used the existing structure. But then a series of really practical issues came in. The silos were quite small boxes, only 2.5 metres wide on either side. Then we talked about ideas where we might do the servicing through them or the lifts!

Sune Nordgren: To go in a lift through a silo – horrible! Keeping the silos was nostalgic thinking. There was too much romanticism around the building.

Dominic Williams: We still had pillars in when Sune arrived. People found it very difficult to let go. It is endemic in a lot of these industrial buildings, where people keep elements and they become isolated. They almost become strangers in their own land, so to speak.

Sune Nordgren: And then they brought in this horrible Swedish minimalist who took out the last remaining elements of the old building! I think keeping the original features would have given us a problem actually, because you would have had a building that was constantly present. When you looked at the art in the galleries, you'd have these sentimental references to the old building. The inside of BALTIC is a rational building for the user.

Jane Rendell: This sounds very Swedish to me! There is a strong strand in Swedish design of a rational and human modernism, along the lines of architect Gunnar Asplund perhaps?

The Stockholm City Library is probably Asplund's most famous work and could be described as one of the first pieces of architecture to combine classical forms and rational thinking with humanist ideals on a fairly intimate scale. In this sense, BALTIC is very modern. It is not trapped by history; it is a building looking forward. This seems a very important aspect of the design: the desire to look towards the future, not to be nostalgic and turn towards the past.

Dominic Williams: There are much more, shall we say, subtle things going on than the obvious thing of keeping a piece of the original building. For instance, the whole structure of the building still follows the original 2.5 metre x 2.5 metre grid of the silos. You can see this in many of the ceiling lighting grids. Another idea we had, which didn't happen in the end, was to keep the memory of the original grid layout through light crosses on Baltic Square. But most importantly, BALTIC is still a building about 'process'.

Jane Rendell: The silos are clearly an important part of the building's history, and have been key to debates about heritage and so on, but I was also thinking more about the design potential that their vertical nature offered.

Dominic Williams: We talked about retaining an essence of what the silos were like. Although the building has been re-orientated from a vertical to a horizontal axis, I think that in some sense the vertical feel has been retained, certainly in terms of the way you move through the building. You can either go up in the lifts or you can go up a staircase through one of the main vertical cores of the building. Some people will want to experience these spaces, some people might not! I remember when we first got in the building, you had to take a rickety ladder right up one of the silos. I thought it was important that some of that experience was retained in the new building. When we first arrived at the top of the building in a low space above the silos, I was shocked to find so many dead birds. How did they get in? Then I realised it was through the creaking silo vents above our heads.

Level 5 – The Viewing Box:
'dinosaur museum'

Jane Rendell: Whenever I go to a new place I like to take in a view from the highest point first, although this has taken a different turn somehow since the events of 11 September 2001. Michel de Certeau even wrote an essay from the top of the World Trade Centre, where he makes an interesting connection between looking and knowing. He describes the difference between looking down from on high, where you get the feeling that you know somewhere in a detached sort of way, from the way you get to know a place on the ground, completely immersed in what's happening. A position of detachment allows uninterrupted vision. It brings to mind the notion of 'a vision'. When you're up high, looking out, you can imagine all kinds of different possibilities. Where did the vision of BALTIC begin?

Dominic Williams: BALTIC has had a long history and a lot of people have been involved in the project over the years. For me, it really started with Gateshead Council and meeting the Mayoress, Councillor Pat Murray, now a BALTIC Trustee, in 1994. They said, 'You've won the competition and we want it ready by '96!'

Jane Rendell: Was the building intended to be a space for art from the beginning?

Dominic Williams: There were lots of different ideas: offices…

Sune Nordgren: …a hotel, residential homes even…

Dominic Williams: …even a dinosaur museum! And that was after we started the design! This was around the time of the release of the film *Jurassic Park*. It was before Sune came on board.

Sune Nordgren: But when I arrived it was still a dinosaur museum in a way! Because people in the arts community here had very mixed feelings about BALTIC. Of course, they welcomed the possibility of having an international centre for contemporary art in the North East, but they were also scared there would just be this very big, heavy institution crushing everything else, sucking out all the resources of the region. There was a very mixed feeling about it, so it was a kind of 'dinosaur' that suddenly arrived on the art scene! This is why we set up the pre-opening programme, to provide the opposite. There are a couple of things that have always been in the design though. For example, the viewing box: Dominic recognised from very early on that there would be beautiful views from up here.

Dominic Williams: The viewing box is a place where you can observe and be observed, and I thought that was important.

Jane Rendell: People are used to seeing the *Angel of the North* as they approach Gateshead; but now we have a glimpse of the BALTIC viewing box. It gives you a real clue that something has changed.

Sune Nordgren: As Dominic says, it's a place where you will actually be seen because the east and west façades are open – completely glazed – so you will see people walking, going up and down in the lifts and so on. And there's no façade lighting: all the light will come out of the building instead, so you will really see that it's a busy place.

Jane Rendell: I think it seems to be quite a key element of BALTIC: that you can be inside and immersed, but you can also travel up the building to the top and take in the view right over Gateshead and Newcastle.

Dominic Williams: To the left you can see Gateshead Car Park designed by Owen Luder [currently under threat of demolition]. It was used in the film *Get Carter* in the famous scene where they chucked the architect off the roof!

The Restaurant:
'as if something has landed on top of the building'

Dominic Williams: I remember standing on the roof at the time the Lottery money was awarded in 1997. There was a brass band and all their hats and things were blown off the top of the building! We knew then that to enjoy the view, a place on the top would have to be enclosed.

Sune Nordgren: You had a fantastic idea about this restaurant early on: that it would be built on the ground and then brought up with a crane and put in place on the roof. And you could actually take it on and off again if you wanted!

Dominic Williams: The original brief in 1994 asked for a temporary exhibition space and a café. This led to the idea of a moveable café on the forecourt that could be lifted into position as a big event for the Visual Arts Year in '96! The local newspaper called it 'Pie in the Sky'!

Jane Rendell: It does appear from a distance as if something has landed on the top of the building.

Sune Nordgren: Yes, it's basically a glass box.

Dominic Williams: The question was: how could we have a space where you could enjoy the view but also get light down into the gallery space? So the structure evolved from that requirement, but it had to be lightweight as well.

Sune Nordgren: The Rooftop Restaurant will be run, together with the Riverside Restaurant and the café-bar in the Riverside Building, by the McCoys, who own the Tontine restaurant in North Yorkshire and have a very good reputation in the region.

'To take a monolith, a great slab of a building, and transform it into a piece of static art, is to erect a monument to those who conceived it.

Oft seen, but rarely recognised, BALTIC now stands in the sunshine and dignifies those who live by the Tyne. BALTIC will never really exist till it happens and then I hope it can't be truly defined. Just loved.'

Tom McCoy, April 2002

East Viewing Box:
'excluding half of humanity!'

Sune Nordgren: There are things in the building I think people will talk about and this, the view from the ladies' toilets on Level 6, is one of them. These kinds of things create a story around the building.

Jane Rendell: The views are incredible. I do enjoy being given this grand view to look at when I wash my hands.

Sune Nordgren: And it's just for ladies – terrible isn't it? Excluding half of humanity!

Jane Rendell: But what is even more interesting is how this very private space, which is usually hidden away at the back of a building, is put on view here. Perhaps it's the transgressive part I like.

Dominic Williams: Behind those new flats on the Newcastle Quayside you can see the Byker Wall poking out just above the skyline. This was a scheme designed and built over a long time, from 1969 to 1981; I remember it very clearly from when I studied architecture. A place where people could influence the way the architecture developed. Ralph Erskine, the architect of Byker Wall, let people influence the design of their own homes. We are trying to do a similar thing in BALTIC: to create a volume or space where the people coming in to use it can have quite a lot of freedom within it. I am interested in that kind of social architecture.

Sune Nordgren: Also in the tradition of Erskine, Dominic thought very early on of green, low-energy solutions for BALTIC. We wanted this to be a place that had a good reputation for being environmentally friendly. We looked, at one stage, of heating the whole place with the energy from the tide in the Tyne.

Dominic Williams: We also had ideas about how we could use the river for cooling, for sprinkler tanks and for creating energy for the lifts.

Sune Nordgren: In some cases, there were issues in terms of the maintenance of these systems that meant that they didn't make it into the final design.

Dominic Williams: We had a limited budget. But what we have done is create a lot of low-energy solutions. You can look down now and see the energy centre. Having the main plant in a separate building means that it can run for twenty-four hours, so it's called 'combined heat and power'. This unit runs on gas, which is a good, clean energy. In addition it provides the electricity for BALTIC. If the power is not being used, it can be sold back to the National Grid, so it helps keep the running costs low. We had to insulate the building quite a lot, and obviously having a lot of solid wall helped: it meant we could emphasise the areas between the solid walls as well and put glass there.

Sune Nordgren: The energy centre is a brilliant solution in terms of space: it means that you can take plant out of the main building, leaving 80 – 85% of the main building for the purpose it should be used for…

Dominic Williams: …for art.

Looking Down into Level 4 Art Space:
'between looking at art and looking at the city'

Dominic Williams: I think places like this, with views out, are very important. People can just stand here, look out and think about something else, or nothing at all.

Jane Rendell: Yes, this seems to fit with the idea of taking time in BALTIC. It's interesting to think about the state of mind we view art in. We often think of it as a focused and contemplative kind of looking, whereas the way in which we experience other spaces and objects, outside in the city for example, is often in a state of distraction. Is there a difference between looking at art and looking at the city?

Dominic Williams: It's also important that there is always a choice of routing in BALTIC, so that people can reconnect with the view outside and the Tyne Bridge. These views suddenly remind people of where they are.

Sune Nordgren: Especially for the opening, with Chris Burden's Meccano Tyne Bridge, which will be seen in relation to the actual Tyne Bridge, visible through the gallery window.

Jane Rendell: The relationship between 'the gallery' and the world outside seems vital to the design and use of BALTIC and raises questions such as: how are the works of art inside the gallery related to the city outside? Are they separated or connected? Does their relationship change depending on where you are in the building?

The Secret Space:
'it's a bit like the film 'Being John Malkovich''

Jane Rendell: Why do you call this particular room the 'secret space'?

Sune Nordgren: It's not really on a floor, it's in between Levels 3 and 4.

Dominic Williams: It's a bit like the films *Being John Malkovich* or *Brazil*: it's kind of in between floors A and B! We didn't know we had it until we started looking at the drawings and setting out all the levels.

Jane Rendell: Did you have to do survey drawings for the building?

Dominic Williams: The building was already surveyed but when the silos came out, we had to re-measure the interior to check that everything fitted. It's quite important, always checking measurements. It's an ongoing process when you're working with an existing building.

Jane Rendell: There are different kinds of drawings: really precise drawings that convey accurate information, and more inspirational drawings. Have drawings been important in the design process or have you worked more with models?

Dominic Williams: We've used them all: computers, models and drawings. But it started very simply with sketches and concepts. Early on we used sections, where you can really look at the sort of volumes you've got inside. It wasn't possible to read those volumes when the silos were in. So it was very difficult to imagine the spaces we have now. I remember the engineer Chris Correa leaping enthusiastically into a cat's cradle. A worker at Baltic Flour Mills would have been lowered down a silo through a small hole at the top. It took us half an hour to get him out!

Level 4 Art Space: 'it's enormous!'

Jane Rendell: From the outside BALTIC has a grand and imposing structure, but inside, even though the spaces are really generous, they're not overpowering.

Sune Nordgren: It's enormous! This space is very high, 8.5 metres to the ceiling, but it has a human scale. It will probably be used by the artists in an open way.

Jane Rendell: Is that the arts lift, over in the corner?

Dominic Williams: Yes, another important aspect of the design was the movement of work and materials, as well as people, through the building. From very early on, we thought that the arts lift needed to be big enough to move materials directly into the main gallery spaces and loaded easily at the bottom of the building.

Jane Rendell: What about the weight of work that can be carried?

Dominic Williams: The maximum weight calculated was for a total live loading of ten tonnes.

Sune Nordgren: And the point loading of the galleries is six tonnes.

Dominic Williams: The structure is designed, certainly if you go down to Level 3, to be able to hang point loadings from the ceiling as well as support very heavy works.

Jane Rendell: There is a long tradition of artists intervening in the fabric of the gallery, pushing galleries right to their limits. What about if an artist wanted to cut into the fabric of the building itself?

Sune Nordgren: They could. The material is not very prestigious: it's quite simple, replaceable. So is the wooden floor. It's like working in any other industry or workshop. You can drill, bang nails into it or whatever. If it's really badly treated for a while, you can just sand it

down and then you have a new floor again. It's a very, very strong wood called 'gammelskog' which in Swedish means 'the old forest'. The trees are between 150 and 200 years old. We had questions from English Heritage: 'can you take so much of this wood without actually destroying the forest?' It's no problem, but it took the supplier more than two years' worth of supply to provide us with the wood we needed, because they couldn't take it all in one go.

Level 4 Roof Terrace: 'the kittiwake story!'

Jane Rendell: Questions of heritage and the environment really enter BALTIC by way of the kittiwakes, don't they?

Dominic Williams: Oh God, the kittiwake story! Where shall I start? Well, originally we had a nesting population of kittiwakes on the side of the building. So we had to deal with the kittiwakes, a protected species of bird. We had to make a temporary structure beside the building to attract them. One proposal was made by an artist and bridge-maker called Richard La Trobe-Bateman. Everybody was very sceptical, but when the building was netted, all the kittiwakes moved and lived on this temporary structure!

Sune Nordgren: Ninety couples were nesting there last year.

Dominic Williams: The structure was moved down-river because of health and safety risks. So we've now had to create a number of special ledges on the building to try to prevent kittiwakes from nesting.

Sune Nordgren: Dominic also looked into different techniques: for example, seeing if you could scare them away with the sound of birds of prey, which isn't audible to the human ear.

Dominic Williams: Apparently it would have worked on any other bird apart from kittiwakes! The person we consulted also advises all the airports. He said, 'You've got kittiwakes – no chance! We tried. Even sonic booms wouldn't get rid of them.'

Jane Rendell: It's nice to be so near to the 'Baltic Flour Mills' lettering here. It looks striking from a distance and up-close you realise the scale of it. The letters are almost two metres high.

Sune Nordgren: There was a discussion about whether we should keep the text on the façade. The words don't really make sense anymore because it isn't the 'Baltic Flour Mills', it's 'BALTIC'. But they're such a strong feature – beautiful tiles and in great condition – that we decided to keep them.

Orientation Space for Level 3 Art Space:
'between looking at art and not looking at art'

Sune Nordgren: Most artists will see the orientation spaces, like this one, as the start of the gallery. The orientation space can be used for different things. You can put a coffee bar or a mobile bookshop here, for example.

Jane Rendell: Yes, I find these kinds of spaces, just on the edge of the so-called 'galleries' themselves, very interesting. What state of mind are we being asked to adopt inside buildings like BALTIC when we are not looking at art in the galleries? Are we being prepared to look at art? Or are we being offered alternative occupations, a view of the city to look at or a cup of tea to drink? BALTIC seems to be a place that plays with these different relationships, particularly in a space like this that is placed right between looking at art and not looking at art. It is not a café or a bookshop, nor are we in a designated 'gallery', so where are we? Is this a place where we can have a more relaxed relationship with the artists?

Sune Nordgren: Yes, many artists today are very interested in interacting with the public, but sometimes they feel they can't really do it in a gallery space because it's so defined: anything you put in there becomes 'art'. You want to meet the public in completely different kinds of spaces.

Dominic Williams: We always looked at the structure in terms of its potential to allow this to happen: from classic white boxes through to those very open spaces that interact with them.

Level 3 Art Space:
'it is not a museum'

Jane Rendell: There is certainly a real combination of art spaces in BALTIC, from Level 4, which is big and light, to Level 3, which has a lower ceiling and is more intimate.

Sune Nordgren: People are surprised when they walk around the building – the spaces are so different. In one way, Level 3 is easier to use than upstairs because it is possible to make partitions here. It has beautiful, very good proportions. It is also the only level that has close control in terms of climate and lighting, and it can be closed off as a 'black box'. But I remember a discussion with Dominic: 'If this is a place for contemporary art, why do you need a controlled art space? It is not a museum.' But even though BALTIC is a place for contemporary art, we can also take on the possibilities of doing what we call 'anchor exhibitions', where you anchor contemporary art back to modern art or the modern classics.

Jane Rendell: Well, there is also so much crossover today with artists and curators working between the archive, the museum and the art space. Think of the recent 'Give & Take' exhibition between the Serpentine Gallery and the Victoria and Albert Museum in London, which explored the relationship between galleries and museums. The artist Hans Haacke took a number of objects from the Victoria and Albert Museum and repositioned them in the Serpentine Gallery, while a number of other artists made work to be installed in the Victoria and Albert Museum. Then you have artists making interventions into museums and galleries, such as those by Marysia Lewandowska and Neil Cummings, who have critiqued the ways that art institutions operate using the historical categories of an archive as well as the cultural codes and spatial organisation of a museum. You really need to offer the flexibility for being able to display historical artefacts.

Sune Nordgren: I am happy that we have gone away from the so-called 'white cube' situation. Only the ground floor gallery is a white cube. The rest of the spaces have their own individual identity. My experience is that artists want to have some kind of challenge with architecture when they create their art.

Jane Rendell: Something to work against, rather than the same clean canvas.

Level 2 Office Space:
'because I'm worth it'

Jane Rendell: People have described this space for the administrative staff as the heart of the building.

Sune Nordgren: It is pulled back away from the lifts and the art space on the upper level of the second floor, so it is located physically at the heart of the building.

Jane Rendell: Although pulled back from the lifts, this heart is still visible, which suggests to me an idea about social transparency. It is interesting to consider the relationship the administration of BALTIC has physically with the other spaces in the building – the art spaces, the cafés and bookshop and the intermediary spaces – which might be a reflection of a social vision.

Sune Nordgren: Exactly. We like the idea of having this interaction with the public. When you pass in the lifts, you can look into the administration area. The upper level, where staff will do desk-based work, is not sealed off. The visiting public will arrive in the reception downstairs, where there is a library, an archive, the print workshop and the spaces for distribution of mail. So if this is the heart of the building, it is probably the brain of the building, the memory of the building, as well.

Jane Rendell: The second floor has an open-plan layout, indicating again some kind of social aspiration – perhaps a more democratic or flat structure?

Sune Nordgren: We have been discussing various types of working, from everyone having a laptop and a mobile phone, to a very open space where you can configure and reconfigure the seating easily to work on different kinds of projects. So this is something in between a landscaped office and a hot desk situation: an open space where you can move around.

Jane Rendell: I was wondering where gossip might take place? The best chats are always at the kettle or at the photocopier. These are key places for communication, where you give away things by accident.

Sune Nordgren: One of the principles of BALTIC is not to have any coffees at the desks! You have to go down to the staff rest area for a coffee, which is much better, because you leave your work and go and meet someone. A basic problem for all organisations, no matter what their size, is internal information. It is very, very difficult. That's why you have to create these kinds of places, where people meet and share information.

Dominic Williams: The idea is also to give important spaces to the people who are actually in the building most of the time. And nice working spaces for the technicians, open spaces with lots of light coming in. In a lot of other galleries, very cramped conditions give way to big public galleries. There is more of a balance within BALTIC between back of house and front of house. I think that's what they all deserve!

Sune Nordgren: Yes, very much so: 'because I'm worth it'!

Level 1 Art Space:
'today you can edit a video from a suitcase'

Sune Nordgren: The Level 1 Art Space has all the facilities that will allow it to be used for performance and live events, as well as exhibitions. The mezzanine next door contains what we call the media lab, which has state-of-the-art audio-visual equipment. This will primarily be for use by artists working at BALTIC, although we also plan to hire these facilities out when they are not being used in-house.

Jane Rendell: How did you go about making design decisions here, given how fast digital technologies are changing?

Dominic Williams: Well, we didn't make decisions on equipment initially, we just made decisions on getting access to the equipment, on service-routes and how you could bring services overhead and drop them down through the ceiling.

Sune Nordgren: Very early on we called this the 'digital suite'. In the brief, this was to be a place where people could come and work with computer-based art. And then of course, as you said, technology changed very rapidly: today you can edit a video from a suitcase. So this space became as open as possible, a kind of workshop. There is one studio, the audio lab, which requires special facilities, and the rest is open and flexible: we will roll trolleys around and put up workstations where needed. You can also do a lot of the work in the galleries.

Dominic Williams: We have two kinds of acoustic enclosures here, one on either side: one has a void in it, which allows you to project on to all the walls. Again, in the original design this space was thought of as a virtual reality 'cave', but since then the technology has moved on.

Sune Nordgren: There will probably be a movable cave pretty soon: six screens that you just put together with flat screen technology. This is a very useful room though. It can be used for installations as well as different kinds of screening.

Dominic Williams: The other acoustically-enclosed space on this level is the cinema, which has space for about fifty seats.

Sune Nordgren: Again, we will have film programmes in collaboration with the Tyneside Cinema in Newcastle, for example, as well as running our own programmes that connect in some way with the exhibitions in the galleries.

Jane Rendell: Can you imagine events like club nights and those kinds of things happening in the Level 1 Art Space?

Dominic Williams: Yes!

Sune Nordgren: Absolutely. We envisage this space – which has a full theatrical lighting rig – being used for everything from live art and performance to multi-media events, screenings, installations and club nights. We want to keep this space as open and dynamic as possible.

Ground Floor Art Space:
'it is not a zoo'

Sune Nordgren: Here is the Ground Floor Art Space. When you come in from the main entrance, this gallery is the first art space you come to.

Dominic Williams: The door here opens straight into a workspace.

Jane Rendell: How many artists do you imagine working in-residence at BALTIC?

Sune Nordgren: Four or five at any one time I think. We want them to stay for a while, of course: at least three months, hopefully six.

Jane Rendell: And they can use the art spaces to show work?

Sune Nordgren: They can use anything. But we will not put pressure on them to have a result. They can lock themselves in the studio for three months and then go back home again if they want to. We are just as interested in the process as the product from the artists-in-residence.

Jane Rendell: Will visitors be able to come in and see artists at work?

Sune Nordgren: Well, it is not a zoo, so it is very much up to the artists themselves. Some are really interested in going out into the community and involving people in the work they are doing here, whilst other artists don't like that at all and you can then perhaps ask them to do an open-studio day twice a year or something like that.

Dominic Williams: What you can read here, on this level, is the way we have divided up the building. And you see the theme running through BALTIC. If you take the line of the towers, which run all the way back, you have very active things, like the bookshop and the café/bar, to the sides, to create bigger spaces in the middle.

Loading Bay:
'art in at the back, people in at the front, and something wonderful happens in the middle'

Sune Nordgren: This is the loading bay for the activities that bring art into the building.

Dominic Williams: You can access the arts lift from in here and also directly from the outside.

Sune Nordgren: It is big enough for a full-length truck to drive in and we can close the steel doors for security.

Dominic Williams: Yes, a truck can off-load at the back and possibly at the side here. There is also some limited storage.

Sune Nordgren: Sometimes you can't get rid of an exhibition immediately, so you have to store it somewhere. Up here, on the mezzanine, is storage for the bigger crates. And you have material – timber, mdf, and so on – for building partition walls in the galleries.

Dominic Williams: This will be another incredibly active part of the whole organisation. We have put a glass façade at the back of the arts lift, so you can see it travelling up and down, which is quite nice because it is usually perceived as the back end of the building. With BALTIC, it's more a case of art in at the back, people in at the front, and then something wonderful happens in the middle.

The Riverside Restaurant: 'the BALTIC experience'

Sune Nordgren: We are now in the restaurant on the top floor of the Riverside Building.

Jane Rendell: At the moment people seem really interested in a 'total consuming environment': food, written matter, art, design and architecture all together. We see this in design magazines like *Wallpaper**, but also in recent changes to art magazines like *Make* and *Contemporary Visual Arts*, where moves have been made to accommodate design and architecture, as well as food. Do you think the design of the restaurants will influence whether people choose to eat here?

Sune Nordgren: Absolutely. The spaces in themselves are so spectacular: the Rooftop Restaurant connected to the viewing box, and this restaurant connected to the terrace. When the sun goes down over Newcastle we actually still have it in Gateshead, so people can sit and have a drink on the terrace. The restaurants are important for us because we really want people to stay in the building.

Jane Rendell: Very like the Oxo Tower in London, where the relation to the river is all important.

Sune Nordgren: People like that. They really want to be along the river.

Jane Rendell: What about the furniture? How does this contribute to the design of the restaurant and to the building as a whole?

Sune Nordgren: It's been very important. It has been specially designed by the Swedish furniture designer Åke Axelsson, who I've worked with before – he's in his early seventies now and is very well established in Scandinavia. He has already shown the BALTIC series in Japan, where they were a fantastic success. So you'll probably see BALTIC furniture, not only in BALTIC, but also in other places around the world. All along we have been talking about the so-called 'BALTIC experience'. This whole experience is generated from the old building, but extended into the design – simple, flexible and honest. The furniture reflects

the same thing: solid wood, steel, aluminium and just a simple polyurethane material in the cushions. Nothing is painted, nothing is covered. It's really the same attitude that I think should run through the whole experience of BALTIC.

Jane Rendell: So, final thoughts. Dominic, this must be amazing for you, to see the project you first envisaged back in 1994 almost complete?

Dominic Williams: Yes it is, but strange in a way as well, to actually see how things have taken shape. We have been with it for so long, so to finally see it happening is almost a shock.

Jane Rendell: Sune, you must be quite excited, getting ready to move in?

Sune Nordgren: Oh, it is fantastic. It will take a while before the BALTIC team learns about the building and how to use it. So I imagine it will take a couple of years before you see the full potential of it.

Dominic Williams: What is good about the opening exhibition is that the artists have left the spaces very much as they are at the moment. That's been really encouraging, certainly for the design team, to see artists coming in and being able to work with the spaces. There are always issues about details, but generally it seems to feel very right. Then I think things will evolve.

Sune Nordgren: And as you said as well, artists will want to challenge the building. Artists always want to challenge, because they are always challenging themselves. Here they are locked into a site with certain conditions and they will want to challenge this.

Dominic Williams: As you said, they might want to drill through the floor.

Jane Rendell: Or they might want to challenge the democratic openness of the administration and start building in, rather than removing, walls.

Sune Nordgren: Yes, but then they would have to get the curator to say 'yes' or 'no'!

'Not one Story but Many': BALTIC Time Line

Where does the 'history' of BALTIC begin? In 1997 perhaps, with the Arts Council's award of Lottery funding for the project, or before this, in 1994, when Dominic Williams was announced as the winner of the architectural competition to convert the old silo building into an arts venue? Or even earlier still, with the closure of the Baltic Flour Mills in the early 1980s? Looking back at the development of the BALTIC project over the years, it is difficult to pinpoint the precise moment of its genesis: perhaps because such a moment never, in fact, existed. The twenty-year progress of BALTIC from disused industrial building to centre for contemporary art is only one part of the 'story' of the art history of the North East, and indeed, could not have taken place at all without those chapters that both preceded and unfolded concurrently around it.

The following time line is an attempt to establish the complex trajectory that led to BALTIC and to acknowledge the input of those individuals and organisations whose work – either directly or indirectly – both paved the way for and contributed to its development. Comprehensive rather than exhaustive, the time line positions BALTIC within the context of the arts activity of the northern region, placing particular emphasis on the work of the local authorities – most notably Gateshead Council and its Public Art programme – and the Regional Arts Board, who together helped create much of the infrastructure that allowed an initiative such as BALTIC to happen in the first place. Another strand running through the time line is the practice of those independent commissioning bodies and artists' groups who, since the 1970s, have played such a crucial role in promoting contemporary art in the region, despite – or perhaps, in part, because of – the absence of a major venue.

The northern region has a strong record for commissioning art for sites outside the confines of the gallery. Somewhat ironically, it is precisely this history that leads us, via the two Tyne Internationals, the Gateshead Garden Festival, Visual Arts UK and the *Angel of the North*, to BALTIC – not one story, but many.

Sarah Martin
Assistant Curator, BALTIC

With thanks to all those who contributed to the time line and assisted with the research,
in particular Sarah Cook/Locus +, Peter Davies, Anna Pepperall, Peter Stark and Paul Usherwood.

The Magpie, illustration from Thomas Bewick, *A History of British Birds, Vol.1, Land Birds*. Facsimile edition of 1797 original, Frank Graham, Newcastle, 1971, pp.92–93.

Thomas Bewick (1753–1828)

Thomas Bewick (born in Ovingham, Northumberland) establishes his own engraving studio in Newcastle in 1797 and lives, from 1812 onwards, in nearby Gateshead.

Known as 'the father of wood engraving', Bewick is celebrated during his lifetime for such works as *A General History of Quadrupeds* (1790) and *A History of British Birds* (1797 & 1804). Through his work, and the distinctive style of the engravers in his workshop, Bewick promotes the idea of Newcastle as an artistic centre independent of London and demonstrates the artistic and commercial potential of the hitherto neglected medium of wood engraving.

The Literary and Philosophical Society

Founded in Newcastle in 1793 with the aim of educating the population of Newcastle and the surrounding areas, the Lit and Phil is a pioneer of scientific invention and discovery in the region.

Housed in a Grade II* listed building in Newcastle, which opened in 1825 to house its collection of academic and non-fiction books and to host scientific demonstrations and lectures.

Today the Lit and Phil is a modern lending library with over 140,000 academic and general non-fiction books.

Thomas Miles Richardson

Dubbed 'Father of the Fine Arts in Newcastle', Thomas Miles Richardson (known for his epic painting *Newcastle from Gateshead Fell*, 1816) organises numerous art exhibitions in Newcastle between 1822–43. (The Northumberland Institute for the Promotion of Fine Arts is based at his house in Brunswick Place from 1822–27; becomes the Northern Academy of Art in 1828 and moves to new premises in Blackett Street.) As a result, a small number of local artists are able to make a modest living, either by selling work or giving drawing lessons, which in turn encourages artists from other parts of Britain to take up residence in the town.

John Martin (1789 – 1854)
Born in Haydon Bridge, Northumberland, living and working in London from 1806, John Martin becomes one of the most celebrated British painters of his day, famous for his grandiose landscapes inspired by classical and religious subjects. Today, many of his works are held in the collection of the Laing Art Gallery, Newcastle. See Paul Usherwood, 'Art on the Margins: from Bewick to Baltic' in *Newcastle upon Tyne: A Modern History*, Robert Colls and Bill Lancaster eds., Phillimore & Co. Ltd., 2001.

William Bell Scott (1811 – 90)
Painter-poet William Bell Scott moves to Newcastle from London in 1844 to take up the post of master of the new Government Design School. (Design Schools are established across Britain during this time to train designers and draughtsmen for local industry.) Famous for his painting *Iron and Coal* (1861), an allegory of the Industrial Revolution first shown in Newcastle, Bell Scott is critical of the traditional teaching methods employed by T.M. Richardson. Bell Scott also introduces Newcastle collector James Leathart to the work of the Pre-Raphaelites and in 1853, entertains Dante Gabriel Rossetti at his Newcastle home.

Fine Art and Mechanical Inventions Exhibition
Held at the Town Hall in Newcastle to raise money for the Mechanic's Institute in New Bridge Street. The exhibition includes Pre-Raphaelite paintings from the collection of James Leathart, which are criticised by the press.

The Central Exchange Art Gallery
A commercial gallery, located in the former corn exchange built by Richard Grainger in Newcastle town centre. Opened in June 1870 by town councillor Thomas Pallister Barkas (1819 – 91) and the woodcarver Thomas Tweedy (1816 – 92), the gallery runs a programme in which didactic or 'highbrow' exhibitions are combined with competitions, light entertainment and public speaking. It plays an important role in the artistic life of Newcastle prior to the opening of the Laing.

1866   **1870 – c. 1895**

Towards the end of the 19th century, Newcastle artists are beginning to organise themselves into efficient exhibiting bodies:

The Bewick Club composed of local artists and advocating the notion of a civic gallery in Newcastle.

Newcastle School of Art affiliated to the College of Science (part of Durham University) and inaugurates a new exhibiting society, **the Art Circle**.

The Pen and Palette Club, founded by Robert Jobling and Thomas Dickinson. Another instigator of the club is the artist Charles W. Mitchell (1854–1903) who organises a series of exhibitions for the Society in the Academy of Arts, Newcastle. His *Hypatia* (1885) is among three of his works in the collection of the Laing Art Gallery.

See E.M. Atkins, 'The Genesis of the Laing Art Gallery, Newcastle-upon-Tyne' in T.E. Faulkner ed. *Northumbrian Panorama: Studies in the History and Culture of North England*, Department of Historical and Critical Studies, University of Northumbria at Newcastle, 1996.

The Laing Art Gallery in Newcastle is opened on 13 October.

The need for Newcastle to establish a civic gallery is first discussed at a public meeting in the Town Hall in October 1899. This is followed, several months later, by an unspecified gift of £20,000 from Newcastle wine and spirit merchant Alexander Laing (1828–1905), which is used to found the Gallery.

The site is acquired in 1901 and in 1903, the Laing Art Gallery Committee is formed comprising nine members but, in spite of some council protest, no artists. The building is designed by Newcastle architects Cackett &

The Laing Art Gallery, Newcastle.
Photo: Courtesy Tyne and Wear Museums Service.

Burns Dick. The first curator is C. Bernard Stevenson, who remains in post for fifty-three years and is succeeded by his son, C. Bernard Stevenson, who runs the Laing for a further twenty-five years.

The Laing's collection includes both fine and decorative arts by artists such as Thomas Bewick, William Holman Hunt, John Martin, Ben Nicholson and Henry Moore. The Gallery also runs a programme of high profile temporary exhibitions of both historical and contemporary art.

The Shipley Art Gallery, Gateshead. Photo: Courtesy Tyne and Wear Museums Service.

The Shipley Art Gallery in Gateshead, designed by Arthur Stockwell, opens to house the collection of Newcastle solicitor J.A.D. Shipley (1822–1909). Shipley bequeaths his collection of 2,500 paintings to any art gallery in Newcastle large enough to house them and offering free admission. The bequest is rejected by Newcastle when many of the works are revealed to be copies, and, according to the terms of Shipley's will, defaults to Gateshead (along with £30,000 towards the building of a new gallery to house the paintings).

Gateshead's Shipley Bequest Committee selects 500 paintings from Shipley's vast collection,

auctioning the rest, and in 1914, construction of the new gallery begins. The neoclassical building, is formally opened by the Mayor of Gateshead on 29 November 1917.

Now part of Tyne and Wear Museums Service, the Shipley is home to a permanent collection of paintings and other artworks, a display on the history of Gateshead, and a gallery for contemporary craft.

For the full story of the Shipley Bequest see Gateshead Council Local Studies online, www.gateshead.gov.uk/ls/shipley and F. W. D. Manders, *A History of Gateshead*, Gateshead Corporation, 1973.

1917

The **Tyne Bridge** (constructed 1925–28) is opened by King George V on 10 October this year. Designed by Mott, Hay and Anderson, the bridge has a main span of 531ft (162m) and is built at a cost of £700,000. The granite-faced towers at either end of the bridge, originally intended to be used as warehouses, are never completed.

See Stafford Linsley, *Spanning the Tyne: The Building of the Tyne Bridge 1925–1928*, Newcastle Libraries and Information Service, 1998.

The **North East Coast Exhibition** held at Exhibition Park, Newcastle. The main purpose of the exhibition, which attracts over 4 million visitors, is to advertise northern industry and regenerate the local economy during a period of economic depression and intense foreign competition. Among the exhibits are the Palace of Engi-

The Pavilion of Fine Art, 1929.
Photo courtesy of the Military Vehicle Museum, Newcastle.

neering, the Himalayan Railway and the Pavilion of Fine Art, the only surviving building from the exhibition, which today houses the Military Vehicle Museum.

See *Images of England: Newcastle-upon-Tyne*, compiled by Peter Hepplewhite, Tempus Publishing, 1999.

The Ashington Group

The Ashington Group of painters first meet and begin to paint together in 1934 in the Northumberland pit village of Ashington. Founded by Robert Lyon, Master of Painting at Armstrong College, Newcastle, as a Workers Educational Association class, the Ashington Group take as their subject matter the everyday life of miners and the mining community. Today, The Woodhorn Colliery Museum in Ashington holds a major collection of their paintings.

See William Feaver, *Pitman Painters: The Ashington Group 1934–1984*. Carcanet Press, 1993.

1928   **1929**   **1934**

Artist and poet **Crozier** born in Gosforth, Newcastle.

Artist **Conrad Atkinson** born in Cleator Moor, Cumbria. (Later studies painting and drawing at Carlisle College of Art.)

Philosopher **Ludwig Wittgenstein** (1889–1951) works at the Royal Victoria Infirmary in Newcastle for one year during the Second World War.

1936   **Late 1930s**   **1940**   **1943–44**

Baltic Flour Mills. Photo courtesy Rank Hovis MacDougall.

Foundation work begins for the **Baltic Flour Mills** in Gateshead. The project is interrupted by the outbreak of the Second World War and construction of the mills continues in 1948.

Kurt Schwitters in the Lake District, 1945. Photo by Ernst Schwitters. Reproduced by kind permission of Sprengel Museum Hannover. © VG Bild-Kunst, Germany.

Artist **Kurt Schwitters** (1887–1948) arrives in Ambleside in the Lake District on 26 June 1945. (Having fled to Britain in 1940 after the German invasion of Norway, and spending seventeen months interned in Hutchinson Camp on the Isle of Man, before being released and moving to London.) While in Ambleside, he produces a number of portraits and landscape paintings and in 1947, begins work on a new Merz construction, the *MerzBarn*, supported by a grant from the Museum of Modern Art, New York. Using found objects gathered on country walks which were embedded into plaster applied directly to the barn wall, Schwitters works on the relief wall, in failing health, throughout 1947. It remains unfinished at this death in January 1948.

The Arts Council of Great Britain is established as an independent government body for developing knowledge, understanding and practice of the arts. A regional office is based in Bessie Surtees' House, an early 18th-century town house on the Newcastle Quayside, now home to English Heritage.

Construction of **Baltic Flour Mills** continues after the Second World War.

Baltic Flour Mills under construction, late 1940s.

October
Artist and Independent Group member **Richard Hamilton** (b.1922) begins teaching at King's College, University of Durham at Newcastle-upon-Tyne (later the University of Newcastle.) One of his earliest projects is to plan the exhibition 'Man, Machine and Motion' (opens May 1955). Among those students to study under Richard Hamilton during this period are Bryan Ferry (born in Washington, 1945; BA Fine Art 1968), later to become the lead singer of Roxy Music, and play-wright David Storey.

1950   **1953**

The **Baltic Flour Mills** opens in Gateshead on a site formerly occupied (until 1889–90) by Gateshead Iron Works, famous for constructing the High Level Bridge in Newcastle. Built for Joseph Rank Limited (who named all their UK mills after seas and oceans) the Baltic Flour Mills is a dual-purpose factory for the production of flour and animal feed. The mill complex is comprised of five buildings, including the silo (later to become BALTIC), where wheat is stored and cleaned before processing in the mill. Several hundred people are employed at the Baltic Flour Mills until its closure in 1982.

'Progression through the mill was fairly lengthy. I started as a cleaner and finished up mill foreman. The process itself – the why's and wherefore's of how you get white flour from a grain of wheat – is very interesting and a lot of work goes into it; it's in your blood. When I was at the mill, I took a lot of pride in what I did.

On the day the mill closed we all got together for a photograph. There was a conviviality, a carnival atmosphere amongst people. Of course, after the photograph was taken it was just a matter of shaking hands and saying goodbye to all your colleagues.'
Ken Miller, Baltic Flour Mills worker 1961–82. From 'Baltic Memories' video, produced by A19 Film and Video for BALTIC, 1999.

Workers outside Baltic Flour Mills, 1969, taken from the Rank Hovis in-house publication *Activity* (Issue 31). Photo reproduced by kind permission of Rank Hovis Limited.

Artist **Victor Pasmore** (1908–98) teaching at Kings College, University of Durham at Newcastle-upon-Tyne.

The same year he is appointed a member of the design team for the New Town of Peterlee, County Durham. Working with the architects Frank Dixon and Peter Daniels, Pasmore's designs for houses seek to create an aesthetic effect through movement rather than static composition. His involvement in Peterlee culminates in the installation of the Apollo Pavilion (in 1970).

Artist and poet **Robin Crozier** studies Fine Art at the University of Durham. Since 1961, Crozier, who becomes increasingly involved with Fluxus and later, mail art, has taught at Sunderland Art College. See catalogue to the exhibition *Live in Your Head: Concept and Experiment in Britain 1965–75*, Clive Phillpot and Andrea Tarsia, Whitechapel Art Gallery, London, 2000.

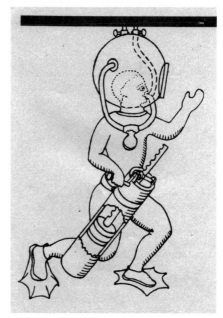

Borelli, *Diving Gear Project*, 1680, from 'Man, Machine and Motion', 1955. Illustration reproduced from the exhibition catalogue, with kind permission of the University of Newcastle Fine Art Library.

1954   **1954–58**   **1955**

May
The exhibition **Man, Machine and Motion** opens at the Hatton Gallery, Newcastle (and later travels to the ICA, London). Selected and designed by Richard Hamilton, the theme of the exhibition-environment is 'man's relationship with the machinery of movement'. It contains over 200 mainly photographic documents of '*machines which extend the powers of the human body in a special way, the machines which increase a man's capacity for autonomous movement.*'

Lawrence Gowing and Richard Hamilton in the preface to the exhibition catalogue, May 1955.

See also *The Independent Group: Postwar Britain and the Aesthetics of Plenty*, David Robbins ed., The MIT Press, 1990.

'an Exhibit' (installation shot), 1957. Photo courtesy of the Hatton Gallery, Newcastle.

June
The exhibition **an Exhibit** opens at the Hatton Gallery in Newcastle.

Conceived and designed by Richard Hamilton and Victor Pasmore, 'an Exhibit' is an environmental exhibition (like the earlier 'Man, Machine and Motion') in which abstract, coloured acrylic panels are arranged in such a way that the spectator can move through them, creating their own compositional groupings:

'*"an Exhibit" is a game, an artwork, an environment; pre-planned, individuated, verbalised by Richard Hamilton, Victor Pasmore and Lawrence Alloway, to be played, viewed, populated.*'

The Independent Group: Postwar Britain and the Aesthetics of Plenty, David Robbins ed., The MIT Press, 1990, p.160.

Northern Sinfonia, the North's professional orchestra, is established.

1957

1958

Richard Hamilton and **Victor Pasmore**, both teaching at Kings' College, Newcastle, collaborate (until 1961) on a joint course in Basic Design, strongly linked to the ideas of the Independent Group. Derived from Johannes Itten's preliminary course at the Bauhaus, the course is intended to be a series of exercises concerned with line, tone, colour, form and space, breaking down the barriers between art, design and architecture.

May
The exhibition **Exhibit 2**, designed by Richard Hamilton and Victor Pasmore at The Hatton Gallery, Newcastle.

North Eastern Association for the Arts is founded by local authorities on 27 April 1961. (Becoming Northern Arts Association in 1967, when Cumberland and Westmorland join.)

Dame Flora Robson is Northern Arts' first President. *'Art is vital to the life of the people, and the North, where I belong, can show this country that art is a large part of our daily lives.'*

By 1962, forty-one local authorities support the new arts association. A grant of £500 is made to the visual arts.

1958   **1959**   **1961**   **1962**

The Animals are formed in Newcastle, when singer Eric Burdon joins the Alan Price Combo. They release their debut eponymous album the same year and go on to become one of the most successful British R & B groups of the 1960s.

March
Connie and **Tom Pickard** take out the lease on The Morden Tower, a 13th-century building in Back Stowell Street, Newcastle, where they initiate the celebrated series of poetry readings and performances that continues to this day. The first reading, by Pete Brown, takes place on 16 June and over the years, writers including Allen Ginsberg (who gives the first European reading of Kaddish), Ted Hughes, Herbert Read, Seamus Heaney, Angela Carter, Alan Sillitoe, Liz Lochead and Stephen Spender read at the Tower.

'The reading at the Morden Tower altered my own poetic practice slightly toward greater economy of presentation. So I learned more at Morden Tower than I had at a hundred Universities.'
Allen Ginsberg, quoted in The Morden Tower leaflet, 2002.
See *High on the Walls: an Anthology Celebrating Twenty-Five years of Poetry Readings at Morden Tower,* Edited by Gordon Brown, The Morden Tower in Association with Bloodaxe Books, 1990.

The Likely Lads
Written by Dick Clement and Ian le Frenais, 'The Likely Lads' (BBC TV, 1964 – 66) follows the fortunes of two Geordie characters – 'irresponsible' Terry (James Bolam) and 'sensible' Bob (Rodney Bewes) – and goes on to become one of the most successful sitcoms of the 1960s. (Followed, from 1973 – 74, by the follow-up series, *Whatever Happened to the Likely Lads?*)

1963   **1964**

The removal of the *MerzBarn* wall, Elterwater, 1965. Photo: Fred Brookes. Reproduced by kind permission of Fred Brookes.

Due to its increasing state of dilapidation, caused by poor weather conditions and years of neglect, the decision is taken to remove **Kurt Schwitters'** *MerzBarn* wall from its original Elterwater setting. Abbot Hall Art Gallery in Kendal (which had organised a Kurt Schwitters exhibition the previous year) cannot afford to house the wall, which is then offered to the Fine Art Department at the University of Newcastle. Prior to its removal, an extensive survey of the *Merzbarn* is undertaken by **Richard Hamilton**, then a Lecturer at the University, together with three students (one of whom, Fred Brookes, later writes about the operation for an article in *Studio International*, May 1969).

On 22 September the fragile, 25-tonne structure is winched, in one piece, from its original site and taken on a truck to Newcastle, where it arrives on 1 October. It is finally installed in the Hatton Gallery on 21 January 1966, where it has remained ever since.

14 May – 15 June
The Exhibition 'Northeast Group' is held at the Laing Art Gallery, Newcastle. Twenty-nine artists

participate, including Robin Crozier, Fenwick Lawson, John Crisp, Alan Williams and Jim Smith.

22 December
Northumbrian poet **Basil Bunting** (1900–85) gives the first reading of his poem *Briggflatts* (published by Fulcrum Press, 1966) in the Morden Tower, Newcastle.

The following year he receives an Arts Council Bursary and retires from the Newcastle Evening Chronicle, where he had worked as a sub-editor since the mid-1950s.
For a biography of Bunting see *Myers' Literary Guide to the North East*, 2nd Edition, 1997, pp. 38–41.

Northern Arts:
Roy Nicholson is appointed first Visual Arts Officer; a gallery is opened in the offices in New Bridge Street, Newcastle; an Exhibition Officer (Ian Barker) appointed; a regional touring exhibition service established and major exhibitions initiated; a **Northern Arts Collection** started and the basis of visual arts support and infrastructure created.

Northern Arts Literary Fellowship established at Durham and Newcastle Universities. Tony Harrison is the first holder.

Artist **Li Yuan-chia** (1929–94) leaves London and settles in Cumbria, where he remains until his death in 1994.

Publication, by Fulcrum Press, of **Basil Bunting**'s *Collected Poems*. He is appointed to the Northern Arts Poetry Fellowship (1968–70) at the Universities of Durham and Newcastle.

Newcastle Civic Centre (designed by George Kenyon) opened by King Olav V of Norway. The numerous contributions from artists and craftspeople include two large abstract murals by **Victor Pasmore** in the rates hall.

Mid 1960s – early 1970s   1967   1968

Welfare State International is founded by John Fox, Sue Gill (and others).

Now based in the Lanterns House – a Centre for the Celebratory Arts – in Ulverston, Welfare State is a collection of radical artists and thinkers who explore issues of celebratory art and spectacle. See www.welfare-state.org

Amber film and photography collective is established in Newcastle, with the specific aim of creating a film and photographic practice in relation to the working-class communities of the North East of England. Throughout its 30-year history it has pioneered experimental partnerships between filmmakers, photographers, writers and local communities in the North East. Amber films include *Like Father* (2001), *The Scar* (1997), *The Writing in the Sand* (1991) and *Seacoal* (1985).

Amber's extensive photographic collection includes work by renowned documentary photographers such as Henri Cartier-Bresson, Weegee, Robert Doisneau and August Sander. The Amber collective also runs the Side Gallery, a Study Centre housing the archive of the Independent Workshop Movement and has a 53-seat 16mm cinema on its premises in Newcastle. See www.amber-online.com

Mike Tilley and Norma Pickard set up the **Whitley Bay Photography Centre**.

Chris Carrell founds **Sunderland Arts Centre**.

Byker Wall, Newcastle, designed by Ralph Erskine.

The redevelopment of the **Byker Estate** in the East End of

Photo: Peter Fawcett.

Newcastle is one of the first major attempts in Britain to create a dialogue between architecture and the community. Architect Ralph Erskine oversees the development of this famous project, which is carried out in consultation with local tenants.

'Variety of scale and form, texture and colour, are the visible signs of the architect's high regard for the human part of the equation, which makes good housing.'
See Nikolaus Pevsner and Ian Richmond, *The Buildings of England: Northumberland*, Penguin, 1992, p.117.

The **Theatre in the Forest** is opened at Grizedale in the Lake District.

Tim Head, BA Fine Art, University of Newcastle.

Trinity Square Shopping Centre with Gateshead Car Park in the background.

Trinity Square Shopping Centre and Car Park
(designed by architect Owen Luder) built in Gateshead Town Centre.

As the project is completed, signs of movement are detected and the opening of the concrete car park building is delayed for several years until the old mine workings underneath are made safe. The car park is finally opened in the early 1970s, although the structure on the top floor, originally designed as a restaurant, is never finished. In the years following its construction, the fabric of the building begins to decline and in 2001 a decision is taken by Gateshead Council to demolish the car park as part of the regeneration scheme for Gateshead Town Centre.

Late 1960s – early 1970s

Pasmore Pavilion, Peterlee (detail) by Victor Pasmore.
Photo by John Pasmore.
Reproduced by kind permission of John Pasmore.

Completion of **Victor Pasmore**'s 'Apollo Pavilion' in Peterlee New Town. The pavilion, which acts as a bridge over the Sunny Blunts stream, is named after the US moon-landing programme of the time.

The Chaplaincy to the Arts and Recreation in North East England converts a former rectory in Teeside into a centre for artists to meet and work together. The centre includes provision for an Artist-in-Residence.

Vince Rea opens the **Bede Gallery**, Jarrow, converted from an old Second World War communications bunker (closed 1997).

March – April
Richard Hamilton has a retrospective exhibition at the Tate Gallery, London.

Newcastle City Library, designed by Basil Spence, opens.

Summer
Li Yuan-chia meets the painter **Winifred Nicholson** (1893– 1981), living in a farmhouse near Hadrian's Wall, Cumbria. Winifred Nicholson first moved to Cumbria with her then husband, the artist Ben Nicholson, in 1924, returning many times during her life, eventually retiring there.

'You're a big man, but you're in bad shape. With me it's a full-time job, now behave yourself.'
Release of the film **Get Carter** (dir. Mike Hodges, 111 mins) starring Michael Caine as London gangster Jack Carter, who returns to the North East to investigate the murder of his brother. Filmed on

1970

1971

location in and around Newcastle, *Get Carter* uses Gateshead Car Park as the location for one of its most famous scenes.

A re-make of the film, with Sylvester Stallone in the role of Jack Carter, is released in October 2000.

Painter **Sean Scully**, BA Fine Art, University of Newcastle

Photograph by Li Yuan-chia.
Reproduced by kind permission of the Estate of Li Yuan-chia.

August
Li Yuan-chia buys a run-down farmhouse from Winifred Nicholson and converts and extends it to establish the **LYC Museum & Art Gallery** at Banks on Hadrian's Wall, Cumbria. Over the course of ten years (until its closure in 1982) LYC shows the work of over 300 artists and poets including Andy Goldsworthy, Joel Fisher, Winifred Nicholson, Paul Neagu, Bill Woodrow, Roy Fisher and Frances Horowitz, and attracts 30,000 visitors a year.

Basil Bunting becomes Northern Arts President.

Whitley Bay Photography Centre becomes **Spectro Arts Workshop**. Run by Mike Tilley and Norma Pickard, Spectro is based in Whitley Bay until 1976, when it moves to Bells Court in Newcastle.

Northern Arts and the **Scottish Arts Council** organise 'Futurismo 1909 – 1919': an exhibition of Italian Futurism at the Hatton Gallery, Newcastle, which tours to the Royal Scottish Academy, Edinburgh.

Exhibition of the work of **Robin Crozier** ('Retrospective 1936 – 72'), at the Bede Gallery, Jarrow.

1972

IRON Press is founded by Peter Mortimer to champion new poetry and fiction from the North East and beyond. From its base in Cullercoats, North Shields, IRON Press publishes up to five books a year as well as organising launches and other events. They are the first publisher to publish the work of writers including David Almond (who later goes on to win the Whitbread book of the year for his children's novel *Skellig*) and poet Simon Armitage. More recent titles published by Iron Press include *Biting Back* (2001), a collection of new fiction from North East writers and *Voices of Conscience: Poetry from Oppression* (1997).

First **Cleveland International Drawing Biennial**.

Northern Arts organises 'Cezanne: Watercolour and Pencil Drawings' at the Laing Art Gallery, Newcastle; tours to the Hayward Gallery, London.

Conrad Atkinson appointed first Northern Arts Visual Arts Fellow (1974–76).

Northern Arts Gallery
Exhibition Programme 1974–76 includes:
- 'Women, Sexuality and Socialism'. A contemporary feminist exhibition, including Mary Kelley's *Post Partum Document,* curated by Margaret Harrison.
- 'Work, Wages and Prices': an exhibition by Conrad Atkinson relating to low-paid workers including nurses, agricultural and railway workers.
- 'Coal Mining' curated by David Brown in association with the National Union of Miners, including works by artists from the region, notably the Ashington Group.

1973

1974

Wendy Brown and **Brian Hooey** curate the first of three annual international artists' video exhibitions, as part of their three-year residency at Biddick Farm (now Washington Arts Centre).

The **Shipley Art Gallery**, Gateshead, establishes crafts focus programme and crafts collection.

John Hilliard is appointed Northern Arts Visual Arts Fellow (1976–78) and has a culminating fellowship exhibition at the Laing Art Gallery.

Stuart Brisley undertakes a twelve-month Artist Placement Group Residency at Peterlee, supported by the Peterlee Development Corporation. 'The Artist Project', an oral history and photographic archive of Peterlee provided by the people themselves, is exhibited at Northern Arts Gallery.

Group photo of the Basement Group, c.1978. © Locus+ Archive.

The Basement Group, Newcastle, 1977–84. Artists' collective established by a group of artists and students at Newcastle Polytechnic (now the University of Northumbria). The Basement Group (so-called because of its base in a warehouse basement) organise over two hundred live and time-based

1975   **1976**   **1977**

A serious fire in the Blue Cross Mill (where animal feed is stored) causes £500,000 worth of damage to the **Baltic Flour Mills** factory. In the years following the fire, falling sales lead to redundancies.

events during the five years from 1979–84, including Stuart Brisley, Bruce McLean, Mona Hatoum, Judith Barry and Andre Stitt. Basement Group members from 1977 include Jon Bewley (Projects UK; Locus+), Richard Grayson (Artistic Director, Sydney Biennale, 2002), Belinda Williams, John Kippin, Ken Gill and John Adams.

1977–78

Robert Self Gallery, Newcastle. Robert Self, supported by Northern Arts, runs an exhibition gallery as an extension of his London commercial gallery. The gallery is situated near Newcastle's High Level Bridge and shows work by artists such as Gilbert and George, Victor Burgin, Carl Andre and Mario Merz.

Three galleries, **Robert Self**, **Spectro Arts Workshop** and **Northern Arts**, join forces to initiate '1977 – Current British Art'. The artists *'largely share a background of having been concerned, first with the history and structure of the "languages" of art, and subsequently with the ideological content of these "languages" (and others), in the context of art and culture in general. This has brought all of them into positions where socio-political issues are central to their current work.'*
John Hilliard in *Newcastle Writings*, published by Robert Self, 1977.

Participating artists: Victor Burgin, Conrad Atkinson, Art & Language, John Stezaker and Terry Atkinson.

The **Side Gallery** opens in Newcastle. Run by Amber, the gallery runs a programme of documentary photography, including exhibitions by Chris Steel-Perkins, Martin Figura, David Lurie, Graham Smith and Sirkka-Liisa Konttinen.

The exhibition, **The Genius of Thomas Bewick**, is held at the Laing Art Gallery, Newcastle.

20 October – 10 December
'**Art of the Invisible**': an exhibition exploring the impact of theosophy and occultism on modern art, The Bede Gallery, Jarrow.

Northern Arts propose the idea of sculpture residencies in Grizedale Forest in the Lake District and curate the programme for ten years. The first residencies in the 6,000 acre working forest are held by sculptors David Nash and Richard Harris. Since then, over ninety sculptures have been commissioned for the forest and Grizedale has become an influential centre for art in the environment, with up to ten artists-in-residence each year.

1977

Gateshead and Grizedale have strong links, with many of the early Grizedale sculptors being chosen to work on public art commissions in Gateshead, including Richard Harris, Andy Goldsworthy, Andy Frost, Mike Winstone, Colin Rose and Sally Matthews.

Sheila Armstrong elected President of Northern Arts.

Northern Arts Fellows are John Hilliard (Visual Arts), Ros Conway (Crafts), David Lyons (Photography), William Martin (Playwright) and Edward Bond (Literature).

Northern Arts advocates Exhibition Payment Right (EPR) to artists in the UK and initiates an EPR scheme for galleries in the northern region.

This is taken up by some other Regional Arts Associations and later, through the Arts Council, becomes a national scheme.

Anita Pate and **Jennifer Stevenson** are appointed Glass Artists-in-Residence at Sunderland Polytechnic.

Hugh Adams is Critic-in-Residence at Newcastle Polytechnic.

ASPECTS: A Journal of Contemporary Art is established.
Editors Anne and Colin Painter

Yorkshire Sculpture Park opens in 500 acres of 18th-century landscaped grounds at West Bretton, Yorkshire.

Bloodaxe Books founded in Newcastle by Neil Astley.

An independent literary publishing house, Bloodaxe – now based in Tarset, Northumberland – is one of the most important poetry publishers in the UK.
See www.bloodaxebooks.com

1978

Crafts and Film, Video and Photography Officers employed in the Regional Arts Associations.

Paul Neagu is Northern Arts Visual Arts Fellow (1979–81).

Stephen Proctor appointed Glass Artist-in-Residence at Sunderland Polytechnic.

First Arts Development post created in Gateshead Council. (Ros Rigby appointed Arts Development Manager.)

Artists' Newsletter (now [a-n] MAGAZINE) initiated by North, North West and Yorkshire regional Arts Associations as an independent artist-led company, to publish a unique artists' magazine supporting the professional development of visual and applied artists across North and North West England and Yorkshire.

Founded in Sunderland, [a-n] THE ARTISTS INFORMATION COMPANY is based today in Newcastle.
See www.anweb.co.uk

David Dye teaching Fine Art at Newcastle Polytechnic (later University of Northumbria) from

Late 1970s   **1979**   **Early 1980s**   **1980**

1980–1992 (part time) and as Course Leader in MA Fine Art from 1992 onwards.

Artists who have studied Fine Art at Newcastle Polytechnic/ University of Northumbria over the years include Simon Herbert and Jon Bewley (Locus+), Gavin Brown, Richard Grayson, Matthew Higgs, Wendy Kirkup, Hilary Lloyd, Pat Naldi, Paul Stone, Jane Wilson, Daphne Wright, Alexa Wright and Craig Fisher.

Garden Front by **Raf Fulcher**. A sculpture sited outside Jesmond Metro Station in Newcastle, which, together with Keith Grant's three mosaics in Gateshead Metro Station, lead to the establishment

Raf Fulcher, *Garden Front*, 1980. Photo reproduced by kind permission of Nexus.

of the **Art on the Metro** programme of commissions for the Tyne and Wear Metro system.

Other artists commissioned to make art for the Tyne and Wear Metro include Basil Beattie (*Magic City*, Manors Metro, 1987) and Cathy de Monchaux (*The*

Day Before You Looked Through Me, curated by Locus+ for Cullercoats Metro, 1998). See www.nexus.org.uk

'**Who Chicago**', curated by Tony Knipe and Peter Davies: an exhibition showing the work of the Chicago 'image' artists, including H.C. Westerman, Jim Nutt and Roger Brown. The Sunderland Art Centre exhibition tours to Camden Arts Centre and Serpentine Gallery, London; the Scottish National Gallery of Modern Art and the Third Eye Centre, Glasgow.

The Newcastle-based electronic music and performance group

zoviet*france is formed. Their prolific output throughout the '80s and the latter half of the '90s includes *Norsch* (1983), *Popular Soviet Songs and Youth Music* (1985) and *The Decriminalisation of Country Music* (2002).

1981–83
Three mosaics by **Keith Grant** – *Nocturnal Landscape*, *Night* and *Day* – installed at Gateshead Metro, as part of Nexus' Art in Transport Programme.

'Positioned above the end of each platform, the works symbolise the operation of the transport system throughout the 24 hours of each day.'
From the Nexus brochure *Art in Public Transport 1977–2001.*

Gilbert Ward's three-piece stone and copper sculpture is installed in the central courtyard of Darlington Memorial Hospital.

Exhibitions of major 20th-century artists held in the region this year include **Picasso** at the Bede Gallery, Jarrow; **Rodin** at the Hatton Gallery, Newcastle and **Kurt Schwitters** at Abbot Hall Art Gallery, Kendal.

Melvyn Bragg becomes President of Northern Arts.

Peter Fuller, Art Critic-in-Residence, Newcastle Polytechnic.

Paul Neagu's Fellowship work is shown at Sunderland Arts Centre and the Laing Art Gallery.

See *Paul Neagu: A Generative Context*, Paul Overy, Ceolfrith Press, 1981.

Baltic Flour Mills, Gateshead. Photo: Colin Cuthbert.

November
The **Baltic Flour Mills** close after just over thirty years in operation. There are only 170 people employed at the mill by this time. Due to the difficulty and the expense that its destruction would involve, the silo building is the only part of the Baltic factory to escape demolition and remains standing on the south bank of the River Tyne.

Projects UK founded by Ken Gill and Jon Bewley.

The first office-based commissioning organisation in the UK. Over the next ten years Projects UK commissions over three hundred projects by artists including Karen Finley, Stefan Gec, Jana Sterbak and Richard Wilson.

'In 1984 we decided to retire The Basement, in favour of establishing an organisation that was only office-based. We decided we would pursue a strategy where we would have resources that were geared to introducing works to an arena where context, or the site they were presented, were an essential part of how the works were read. That organisation was called Projects UK. Projects UK was the first office-based outfit in this country… Basically we discarded the bricks and mortar. Throughout the eighties we presented events in Newcastle and the surrounding region.'
Jon Bewley, 15 March 2001, from *The Producers* (3), p.96, BALTIC, 2001.

Sculpture North recommends establishing public art projects along the rivers Tyne, Wear and Tees. Gateshead and Middlesbrough take up the challenge: a strategy that echoes the later development of the Tyne and Wear Development Corporation's 'Art on the Riverside' programme.

Drawing in Air: an exhibition of sculptors' drawings, 1882–1982
A Sunderland Arts Centre (later Northern Centre for Contemporary Art) touring exhibition, curated by Tony Knipe. Associated publication with essays by Paul Overy, Dr Terry Friedman and William Packer.

Presences of Nature: Words and Images of the Lake District
Curated by Neil Hanson, this Carlisle Art Gallery exhibition commissions new work from artists and writers including Adrian Berg, John A. Davies, Ian Hamilton Finlay, Raymond Moore, Roger Palmer, Hamish Fulton, Mike Davis, Fay Godwin and Jon Silkin.

Cult Channel 4 music programme **The Tube**, presented by Paula Yates, Jools Holland and Muriel Gray, is broadcast from Tyne Tees Television Studios in Newcastle between 1982–87.

Richard Cole is commissioned to undertake Windy Nook environmental sculpture, Gateshead (installed 1986).

Virginia Bodman is appointed as the first artist in the **Durham Cathedral Artist-in-Residence programme**. Administered since its inception by the Chaplaincy to the Arts and Recreation in North East England, the Cathedral residency seeks to provide time and space for an artist to respond to the Cathedral and for public access to an artist at work. Artists-in-residence since 1983 include Felicity Allen (1984–85), Ian Breakwell (1994–95), Katayoun Pasban Dowlatshahi (1998–99) and Tony Sinden (2001–02).
See www.artschaplaincy.org.uk

Chris Stevens is appointed Artist-in-Residence at Sunderland Football Club. This residency, together with the Durham Cathedral residency and the Artists' Agency's placements, help create the model which was used extensively for the UK Year of the Artist 2000.

Artists' Agency established in Sunderland. The Agency works across the northern region where it seeks to create an awareness of the importance of the arts in society, to initiate new collaborative ventures and to generate opportunities to explore, further develop and broaden people's creative sensibilities. Now re-named **Helix Arts**, the organisation is based in Newcastle.

Andy Goldsworthy awarded Northern Artists' Bursary.

Paul Overy is Critic-in-Residence at Newcastle Polytechnic.

Mike Davies constructs two stained glass windows at Monkseaton Station (*Beach* and *Shipyards*) as part of Art on the Metro.

Photographer **Chris Killip** is commissioned by the Side Gallery to document the work of the sea colliers for a major touring photography exhibition.

Auf Wiedersehen, Pet (ITV, 1983–84)
Television series about the exploits of a group of Tyneside builders working on a construction site in Germany. Written by Dick Clement and Ian le Frenais and starring Jimmy Nail, Tim Healy and Kevin Whately.
A new series, with the same cast, is broadcast on the BBC in April 2002.

May
The conference **Art in Architecture and Landscape** is held at Caedmon Hall, Gateshead.

'**Munch and the Workers**' exhibition opens at Newcastle Polytechnic Gallery.

Kielder Forest Photography Residency established in Kielder Forest, the largest man-made forest in Europe.
John Kippin, Murray Johnson and Richard Grassick are among those artists awarded the twelve-month residency in the early '80s.

Gateshead Sculpture Residency is awarded to Mike Winstone.

Northern Artist Bursary is awarded to sculptor Colin Rose.

Artists' Agency placements in Aycliffe Hospital (Jozefa Rogocki), Darlington Community Care (Stephen Carley), St Hilda's, Middlesbrough (Peter Mountain), Tyne Tees Televison (Ian Breakwell) and Cherry Knowle Hosptial (Suzanne Montgomery).

Basil Bunting (born 1900) dies April 1985.

Gateshead Council establishes an **Art in Public Places' Members Panel** to meet artists and consider proposals prior to their submission to the appropriate committees. The Panel is comprised of the Chair of Libraries and Arts, Planning and Economic Development, and a member of the Conservative opposition.

Creation of **Gateshead Arts Team** – including dedicated post for the Visual Arts (Anna Pepperall is appointed), as well as Arts Officers for Caedmon Hall and Gateshead Borough – with a remit to involve the people of Gateshead in the arts.

Establishment of **The Gallery** at Gateshead Library, to show a range of exhibitions by local and regional artists, as well as touring exhibitions from the South Bank Centre, London.

The **Riverside Sculpture Park** is launched on the Gateshead Quayside as part of Gateshead Council's Public Art Programme, acknowledged as one of the earliest and most ambitious programmes of public art in the country. The Sculpture Park runs along the banks of the Tyne on a previously derelict stretch of land – where iron foundries were once sited – earmarked for regeneration in the early 1980s.

1984

1986

Richard Harris, *Bottle Bank*, 1986.
Photo: Mike Golding, John Kippin,
(Northern Light), 1986.

The first piece to be commissioned is Richard Harris' environmental sculpture **Bottle Bank**.

Built on the oldest part of Gateshead, between the High Level and Tyne Bridges, the work (no longer in existence) consists of a series of stone piers and steel arches echoing the form of the Tyne Bridge as well as making reference to the ships and buildings on the river. Taking four years to complete, the work is unveiled in October '86 by Norman Buchan, Shadow Minister for the Arts, as part of Gateshead's launch of 'Art in Public Places'.

'My aim is to present something that seems to "belong", yet which is outside normal experience.'
Richard Harris, quoted in Paul Usherwood, Jeremy Beach and Catherine Morris, *Public Sculpture of North East England*, Liverpool University Press, 2000, p.67.

Other public artworks unveiled in Gateshead this year:

Windy Nook, a stone sculpture by Richard Cole commissioned by Gateshead Council, is constructed on the site of a former pit slag heap in High Heworth using 2,500 tonnes of granite reclaimed from the old Scotswood Bridge. Built, like Richard Harris' *Bottle Bank*, with help from workers on a Manpower Services Commission scheme and Northern Arts' sponsorship, the sculpture is unveiled in 1986 as part of Gateshead Council's Sculpture Week.

Sports Day by Mike Winstone (1984 Sculptor-in-Residence). A large concrete sculpture inspired by Gateshead's international reputation for sport, situated in Gateshead High Street.

Originally painted red, green, orange and yellow, the work is painted black in 1991 and has remained so ever since.

Window, Colin Rose. A large, stainless steel sculpture on Bensham Bank, Gateshead. Described by the artists as a *'stepping stone between the building and an open space'*, the work suggests the experience of looking through an open window into a garden.

1986

Sculpture Week, Gateshead

A week of events focused on sculpture. Includes Gateshead's first Family Sculpture Day in which members of the public are invited to create their own work under the guidance of a professional sculptor. Sculpture Day, set as the first Sunday in October, goes on to become one of the most popular events in Gateshead's Arts Programme.

February – March
New Work Newcastle '86

The first performance and installation festival in venues throughout Newcastle.

Organised by Projects UK and with contributions from artists including Kathy Acker, Stuart Brisley, Mona Hatoum, Bruce McLean and David Ward.

Artists' Agency receives an ABSA Art award for Artworks in Industry, with artists' placements in Davy Offshore Modules (Julian Cooper), SmithShip Repairers (Len Tabner), Ferguson Industrial Holdings (Valerie Kirk) and British Telecom (Derek Dalton and Bruce Chell).

Amber's film **Sea Coal** wins a major international award at the Munich Film Festival.

One Piece at a Time: a temporary, site-specific installation by **Richard Wilson** in the South Tower of the Tyne Bridge. Commissioned by Projects UK as part of the sculpture project TSWA 3D.

May – June
New Work Newcastle on Tour '87 – Confrontations

The second performance and experimental art festival in Newcastle, with selected works touring to Bradford and Manchester.

June
A World's Waste, Sellafield and Nuclear Reprocessing

A touring exhibition organised by the Brewery Arts Centre, Kendal, resulting from artists' commissions focusing on nuclear industry issues.

Includes Conrad Atkinson's stencilled doormats, curated by Projects UK.

A Bottle of Notes and some Voyages

An exhibition of drawings, sculptures and large-scale projects by **Claes Oldenberg**, with **Coosje van Bruggen**, opens at the Northern Centre for Contemporary Art, Sunderland (touring to Henry Moore Institute, Leeds and The

Serpentine Gallery, London). Following this, the artists are commissioned to make a piece of public sculpture for Middlesbrough town centre.

2D/3D: Art and Craft made and designed for the Twentieth Century

A collaboration between the Laing Art Gallery and the Northern Centre for Contemporary Art. The exhibition and associated conference seek to disturb the rigid compartments in which works of art and craft are set and to focus on materials, production methods and intentions.

November–December
Sculptor **Richard Deacon** wins the Turner Prize.
Established by the Tate Gallery, London, and the Patrons of New Art in 1984. The £10,000 prize is awarded to the person who 'has made the greatest contribution to art in Britain in the previous twelve-months'.

Newcastle Arts Centre is officially opened by Prince Charles as a theatre and exhibition venue in the city centre.

September
Edge88 (First Biennial of Experimental Art)

Curated by Jon Bewley, Rob Le Frenais and Tracey Warr. Includes new commissions from: Rasheed Araeen, Jerzy Beres, Ian Breakwell, Stuart Brisley, Vera Brody, Helen Chadwick, Valie EXPORT, Rose Garrard, Vera Frenkel, Mona Hatoum, Tina Keane, Denis Masi, Alistair MacLennan, Nigel Rolfe, Ulrike Rosenbach, Carlos Santos, Carolee Schneeman, Derek Kreckler/ Adrienne Gama/Sarah Miller, Marcelle van Bemmel, Zbigniew Warpechowski, Paul Wong, Peter Zegfeld, Roberto Taroni, Silvia Ziranek.
Seen in London in August and Newcastle in September.

October–November
New Work Newcastle '88
Includes Alaistair MacLennan, Fran Cottell, Carolee Schneeman and Ulriche Rosenbach.

Mike White is appointed Assistant Director/Arts, Gateshead Council, Libraries and Arts team.

1987

1988

Conrad Atkinson's tribute to iron ore workers, three large cut-out metal and text sculptures, are sited in the town square, Cleator Moor, Cumbria.

All the Cullercoats Pictures, Northern Centre for Contemporary Art, Sunderland (formerly Sunderland Arts Centre).
An exhibition bringing together for the first time the work of Winslow Homer, produced from his Cullercoats studio.

Establishment of **Folkworks**: the development agency for folk and traditional music.

Stormy Monday
Directed by Mike Figgis (born in Carlisle, 1948) and filmed in the North East, the film stars Melanie Griffith, Tommy Lee Jones and ex-Police singer Sting (born Newcastle, 1951).

September–October
New Work Newcastle '89.

Reclamation work begins on the site of the old Teams Colliery overlooking the A1, later to become the site for **Antony Gormley**'s *Angel of the North*.

May
Edge90 (Art and Life in the Nineties)
A Biennale of Innovative Visual Arts. Curated by Jon Bewley, Rob La Frenais and Tracey Warr.

Includes new commissions from Marina Abramovic, Marcelle van Bemmel, Guillaume Bijl, Chris Burden, Keren Finley, Pedro Garhel & Rosa Galindo, Guillermo Gomez Pena, Gwendolyn, Bill Henson, Edwin Janssen, Isaac Julien, Rosie Leventon, Seymour Likely, Black Market, Orlan, Ria Pacquee, Cornelia Parker, Mike Parr, Ben Patterson, Martin Spanjaard, Station House Opera, Mark Thompson and Richard Wilson.

1989   **1990**

Travels to Glasgow (June), London (August) and Rotterdam (September).

September – October
A New Necessity: First Tyne International Exhibition of Contemporary Art.
Curated by Declan McGonagle. International festival of contemporary site-specific art in public locations in and around Newcastle. Includes the Projects UK co-commissions Krysztoff Wodiczko, *Untitled* (a projection on the Tuxedo Royale) and Antonio Muntadas, *where is home?*

May – October
Festival Landmarks '90, The Garden Festival, Gateshead, curated by Isabel Vasseur.
The fourth in the series of Garden Festivals in the UK is held in Gateshead. (Previous festivals had been held in Liverpool, Stoke and Glasgow.) The Festival includes over seventy installations and public artworks by artists, fifty of them specially commissioned, under the heading 'Festival Landmarks '90'. Participating artists include Richard Wentworth (*Meal*, 1990); Elizabeth Wright (*Untitled*, 1990); Tony Cragg (*Raleigh*, 1986) and Phyllida Barlow (*Beneath the Skin*, 1990).

During this period, Gateshead Council earmarks a site in Gateshead for a future landmark sculpture and approaches Northern Arts for funds to select an artist and develop a design.

A number of new artworks are installed in Gateshead's **Riverside Sculpture Park** this year:

Richard Deacon, *Once Upon a Time*, 1990. Photo: Mark Pinder.

Once upon a Time by **Richard Deacon**. Made from painted mild steel, the sculpture is built into the surviving abutment wall of the demolished Redheugh Bridge.

Cone by **Andy Goldsworthy**, built on an old foundry site near the High Level Bridge in Gateshead.

Rolling Moon by **Colin Rose**, originally made for the Glasgow Garden Festival in 1988, and relocated to the Riverside Sculpture Park in Gateshead.

1990

Flower Bed by **David Tremlett** installed in the Riverside Sculpture Park, Gateshead, for the first Tyne International.

'*If you are at all interested in art now and where it is going,*

Newcastle and Gateshead are at the moment the centre of activity. Moreover, what distinguishes this colossal effort is a genuine attempt to wrest art out of the gallery and into our daily lives.'
Marina Vaizey, *The Sunday Times*, 20 May 1990

September – October
TSWA – 4 Cities
North East is host and collaborating organisation for this national sculpture project.

Projects UK commissions four artists to make work for sites in Newcastle:
Chris Burden; **Mona Hatoum**; **Jana Sterback** and **Stefan Gec**.

The **Grizedale Society** wins the £100,000 Prudential Award for the Arts.

The Family by **Gordon Young** unveiled outside Gateshead Civic Centre.
Comprised of three sets of figures depicting familial relationships at different stages in life, the unveiling of the stone sculptures is accompanied by complaints that homosexuality is not represented in the work.

Northern Arts makes a commitment to funding the research and initial costs for a major public artwork in Gateshead. Thus begins the site search and commissioning process which eventually leads, in 1998, to the *Angel of the North* by Antony Gormley.

1991

November
Northern Sights (a company created by the Northern Development Company, Northern Arts, Northern Region Council's Association and Northumbria and Cumbria Tourist Boards) submits the Northern Region's bid to the Arts Council to host The Visual Arts Year in 1996. Emphasising process and based on the concept of 'The Northern Gallery', the bid presents the whole region as a gallery, *'with a magnificent historical collection, a programme of exciting contemporary shows and with artists at work throughout, creating new work.'*
Northern Sight's Chief Executive – appointed in '93–'94 – is Paul Collard.

June – August
Keith Alexander, *A House for Gateshead,* The Avenues Project, 1990–91.
A public art project conceived and led by Artist-in-Residence Keith Alexander in which over 500 local residents and many professional artists are involved in the creation of artworks, furniture and decorative objects for an end-terrace house in Brinkburn Avenue, Gateshead.

Japan Festival Tapestry, by **Alison Wood**, exhibited at the Shipley Art Gallery, Gateshead. Designed and created by weaver Alison Wood to celebrate the twinning of Gateshead Council and Komatsu City Assembly.
Now on permanent display at Gateshead Civic Centre, the tapestry reads, *It is very far from Gateshead to Japan but it is the same sky.*

November – December
New Work Newcastle '91
The last 'New Work Newcastle' festival includes work by Nina Edge and Mike Stubbs, William Easton, John Jordan, Ian Breakwell & Ron Geesin and Roger Ely.

Isis Arts is established. (Founding directors, still with the company, are Clymene Christoforou, Sharon Bailey, Jyl Friggens and Annie Sheridan.) Based at the Buddle Arts Centre in Wallsend, Isis initiates and manages artists' residencies, productions and exhibitions and works with approximately 80 artists a year on collaborative projects. Isis also runs a new media suite for use by artists and arts organisations and manages Artemis, Northumberland's first dedicated Arts in Education agency.
See www.isisarts.org.uk

National Artists' Association (NAA) conference in Newcastle considers Visual Arts Code of Practice and an Artists' Charter.

1991

This year, **Northern Arts** also publishes a document on its policy priorities for the next decade.

'In the Spring of 1991 Northern Arts published a consultation document on its policy priorities for the '90s. It included the ambition to achieve major new capital facilities for the Contemporary Visual Arts and Music in 'Central Tyneside'. As Director of Northern Arts I phoned the recently appointed Head of Libraries and Arts in Gateshead, Bill MacNaught, and told him that 'Central Tyneside' was not code for Newcastle but a reflection of our appreciation for Gateshead's extraordinary work in the Visual Arts in particular. That work having just been celebrated spectacularly during the 1990 Garden Festival, I expressed the personal hope that there might be a building in Gateshead suitable for conversion.'
Peter Stark, Director, Northern Arts, 1984–92.

1991–94
Richard Billingham (2001 Turner Prize nominee) studies Fine Art at the University of Sunderland.

Sustrans – the sustainable transport charity – wins Arts Council/British Gas Working for Cities Award for Art in Public Spaces. Since the late 1980s, Sustrans has commissioned numerous public artworks for the National Cycle Network, including major pieces by Tony Cragg, Andy Goldsworthy, Richard Harris and Sally Matthews on the Whitehaven to Sunderland Coast to Coast Cycleway.

Channel 4 announced as new sponsors of the Turner Prize. The £20,000 prize money is awarded to 'a British artist under 50 for an outstanding exhibition or other presentation of their work in the twelve months preceding 31 May.' The 1991 Turner Prize is awarded to sculptor **Anish Kapoor**.

Sally Matthew's seven metal goat sculptures (*Goats*) installed in the Riverside Sculpture Park, Gateshead.

The northern region is awarded the title of UK Region of the Visual Arts for 1996. (The other competing cities are Glasgow and Bradford.)

Northern Arts becomes one of ten English Regional Arts Boards, supported by the Arts Council, concerned with advocacy, development, support and funding of the arts.

Northern Arts' Purchase Plan

extended to offer interest-free loans to people wanting to commission work from the region's artists and craftspeople.

Peter Davies leaves after almost nineteen years (appointed 1974) as Head of Visual Arts at Northern Arts.

'Many people and institutions have contributed to the achievement of BALTIC. The contributions of some have clearly been essential to particular parts and stages of the process over the years. In our judgement however, the project has only been possible at all because of the extraordinary work of Peter Davies as Visual Arts Officer of Northern Arts during the 1970s

---

1992

Gateshead Council commissions a report from Sandy Nairne and Graham Marchant into the feasibility of converting the Baltic Flour Mills silo building into an art centre.

Other buildings considered for conversion or extension during this period are the Co-operative Wholesale Society Warehouse on the Newcastle Quayside (then owned by the Tyne and Wear Development Corporation and now Malmaison Hotel) and the Laing Art Gallery, Newcastle. As a listed building, with limited floor-to-ceiling heights, the CWS Warehouse is deemed unsuitable for conversion into a contemporary art venue, whilst the Laing, at this time, is constrained by the buildings around it, making expansion difficult.

What, for you, is the defining moment or memory of your involvement with the BALTIC project?

'My first encounter was through the tiny door in the bottom corner of the building, and into the extraordinary space below the chutes which still filled the building almost entirely. Graham Marchant and I were writing a feasibility study. But was it feasible? We climbed up one of the corner towers and as soon as we reached the roof we realised that this building had the best urban view in the North East: that it was a landmark in itself, but would also make the act of looking out over the river, over Gateshead and Newcastle, an event in its own right. And that somehow, if the chutes could be removed, then the space could be released for creative use.

133

and 1980s in building – from almost nothing – the scale, quality, confidence and coherence of the contemporary visual arts constituency in the North.'
Peter Stark, Director of Northern Arts, 1984–92, and Peter Hewitt, Chief Executive, Northern Arts, 1992-97.

In January of this year, the judges for the **1996 Visual Arts Year** visit the North East where they meet local artists on board the Tuxedo Princess.

Zone Gallery established in Central Newcastle by David Sinden and Kate Tregaskis as a leading independent venue for the production, presentation and

Installation shot, Orlan, *This is my Body… This is my Software*, commissioned by Zone Gallery, 1996. Photo: Ravi Deepres.

dissemination of contemporary lens-based and digital media in the North of England. Until its closure in March 1998, Zone runs a continuous programme of exhibitions by emerging and established artists including Andres Serrano, Helen Chadwick, Orlan, Stelarc, John Kippin, Laura Aguilar, Wendy McMurdo and Geoff Weston. (With Michelle Hirschhorn as curator from 1995–98.)

Integration, an exhibition of work by **Andreas Junge**, German Artist-in-Residence at the Bede Gallery, goes on show. His residency, funded by the European festival, is the second in an exchange programme between South Tyneside and Wuppertal.

1992

My second encounter, as Chair of the first meetings of the fledgling trust, was with the spirit of determination that would make this project work. It was a spirit I already knew well in Gateshead, through the Angel and other projects. And although the trustees brought different views and approaches to the project, it was the common determination that was palpable around the table.'
Sandy Nairne, Director, Programmes, Tate.

The exhibition **The Unknown Face of Cuban Art** opens at the Northern Centre for Contemporary Art, Sunderland.

The Newcastle Group exhibit in the Central House of Artists, Moscow, with the show touring to Finland and Latvia.

Stefan Gec, *Natural History*, 1995. Pilgrim Street Firestation, Newcastle.
Photo: John Kippin. © Locus+ Archive.

Jon Bewley and Simon Herbert form **Locus+**: a site-specific visual arts commissioning agency, based in Newcastle, working on the production and presentation of socially-engaged, collaborative and temporary projects, primarily for non-gallery locations. Projects organised since 1993 include Stefan Gec, *Buoy* (1996); Anya Gallacio, *Two Sisters* (1998) and *Repens* (2000); Laura Vickerson, *Fairy Tales* and *Factories* (1999) and Simon Patterson, *Landskip* (2000).

Locus+ also publish artists' books and catalogues, produce multiples and manage the largest archive of time-based work in the UK, consisting of 25,000 images

1993

Krzysztof Wodiczko, *Untitled*, 1990. Large-scale projection on the side of the Tuxedo Royale as part of 'A New Necessity' – the first Tyne International. Photo: Chris Wainwright. © Locus+ Archive.

and several hundred hours of film and video, now housed at the University of Sunderland.

Alan Haydon takes up post as Head of Visual Arts, Northern Arts.

Gateshead Council's **Art in Public Places** Panel, in consultation with the Tate Gallery, Yorkshire Sculpture Park, Northern Arts and the Public Art Development Trust, invite artists to submit proposals for a major public artwork in Gateshead.

September – October
Time and Tide: Second Tyne International

Curated by Corinne Diserens Includes the first Locus+ commission, a broadcast for the Tyne International of the project *Search* by Pat Naldi and Wendy Kirkup.

Pat Naldi and Wendy Kirkup, *Search*, 1993. Surveillance still, Newcastle city centre. Commissioned in collaboration with the Second Tyne International. © Locus+ Archive.

1993

Among the venues is The Co-operative Wholesale Society (CWS) Warehouse on the Newcastle Quayside, housing work by, among others, Rémy Zaugg, Amikam Toren and Shirazeh Houshiary.

The large public sculpture, *Bottle of Notes*, by **Claes Oldenberg** and **Coosje van Bruggen** is installed, as if washed ashore, in Middlesbrough town centre.

The Laing Art Gallery receives £250,000 from the Foundation for Sport and the Arts for its southern extension.

Claes Oldenberg and Coosje van Bruggen, *Bottle of Notes*, 1993.
Photo courtesy Middlesbrough Council.

Jane and Louise Wilson (born Newcastle, 1967) win the Barclay's Young Artist Award.

Northern Arts, English Heritage and Berwick Borough Council set up the **Berwick Gymnasium Fellowship** for artists.

Northern Arts Printmaking franchise awarded to North Shields' Fishquay proposal, later to become **Northern Print Studio**.

1994

Antony Gormley, *A Case for an Angel*, 1989, lead, 77" x 344.5" x 18".
Photo: Anthony Gormley.

January
Artist **Antony Gormley** is selected to produce a landmark sculpture in Gateshead, on the basis of his *Case for an Angel* (1989): a winged lead figure, based on a cast of the artists' body.

Phoenix Cobbles, a cobblestone mosaic by Maggy Howarth installed in the historic area around Toll House, Gateshead, as part of the Riverside Sculpture Park.

Komatsu Artists' Exchange set up, involving two potters from Gateshead – Christine Constant and Jane Hufton – and two from Komatsu in Japan – Junko Tokuda and Shuhei Koshita – with each pair spending time working in the others' country.

The **first annual sculptural lantern procession**, at the Wrekenton and Springwell Estates in Gateshead, organised as part of Gateshead's ongoing Art in Health programme. (Other works created in this programme of arts projects based on health issues, include *The History of Gateshead*, 1988, a 30-metre long mural by Dick Ward; *Sea Piece* and *Ice Flows*, 1990, a stained-glass screen by Mike Davis and Cate Watkinson, and a ceramic mural by Paul Scott – all commissioned for the Queen Elizabeth Hospital, Gateshead.)

November–December
Sculptor **Antony Gormley** wins the Turner Prize.

November
The **National Lottery** is established.
(With 28% of revenue from tickets allotted to Good Causes: Sports, Heritage, Arts, Millennium, New Opportunities Fund.)

1994

Invitation to architectural competition announcement, 1994.

July
A Big Waving Bannerwork by **Bruce McLean**, commissioned for the Tall Ships Race, is displayed on the roof of the Baltic Flour Mills.

Dominic Williams (Ellis Williams Architects, London) wins Gateshead Council/RIBA competition to convert former Baltic Flour Mills, Gateshead, into an international art centre.

'It has always been important to retain as much of the existing character of the fabric as possible, whilst clearly and unambiguously announcing the structure's new purpose.'
Dominic Williams, Ellis Williams Architects.

What, for you, is the defining moment or memory of your involvement with the BALTIC project?

'There are many memorable events over our ten years of championing the project and creating a new cultural institution. From the Channel 4 News interview amongst rats and pigeons in 1994 to the rainbow which framed the building during the lottery assessment.

The defining moment was the decision of Northern Arts to pursue the Baltic Flour Mills, the "Bird in the Bush" rather than the "Bird in the Hand" of the Co-operative building in Newcastle.'
Andrew Dixon, Regional Executive Director, Northern Arts.

Launch of **Northern Arts' Case for Capital** and **Visual Arts UK** at the Tate Gallery, London.

'The Northern Arts "Case for Capital" was a major strategic exercise and publication by Northern Arts to identify the region's capital needs and the strategy for developing them. The proposal for the BALTIC sat within this case for £200m of investment in cultural infrastructure.'
Andrew Dixon, Chief Executive, Northern Arts.

Artist Helen Smith establishes **Waygood Gallery and Studios** in Newcastle with a grant from Newcastle City Council.

Globe Gallery opens in North Shields in May. Founded by Rashida Davison, Globe is an independent contemporary art gallery funded by Northern Arts and North Tyneside Council, organising 6–8 exhibitions a year and 3 single-night Flash-point events.

Northern Print Studio
Officially opened in North Shields by Mary Allen, Secretary General of the Arts Council of England, in 1995, Northern Print Studio is the regional resource for contemporary printmaking, with open-access facilities and technical support for the production of etchings, screen-prints, lithographs and relief prints. The studio also initiates a programme of print publications, commissions, exhibitions and residencies with regional, national and international artists.
See www.northernprint.org.uk

UK Region of the Visual Arts 1996 (Visual Arts UK)
A national, year-long visual arts festival hosted by the North of England which aims to provide new opportunities for artists and to leave a legacy of improved facilities for exhibition and production across the region. The need for a major new contemporary art space in central Tyneside is at the centre of these ambitions:

'Northern Arts considers the Baltic Flour Mills to be of primary strategic importance to the arts in the North of England. It confirms the region's determination to play a part on a national and international platform. The Baltic Flour Mills stands at the centre of the region's planning

1995

1996

Defining Moments:
'Weds 16 November 1994: Peter Hewitt (then Director of Northern Arts), Bill MacNaught and I met for a drink to discuss what assistance Gateshead Council needed to make an application to the Arts Council for a feasibility study for the Baltic Flour Mills. The hope, at that time, was to get a major grant of £20 million by the summer of 1995 and have the project open by November 1996 as the final act of the Visual Arts UK 1996 celebrations.'
David Powell, David Powell Associates Ltd.

for the inheritance from Visual Arts UK 1996.'
Peter Hewitt, Chief Executive, Arts Council of England, then Chief Executive of Northern Arts, quoted in the Overview document produced by Gateshead Council following the Lottery application to the Arts Council in November 1996.

March – May
Antony Gormley's *Field for the British Isles*, comprised of 40,000 terracotta figures, is installed at Greenesfield BR works in Gateshead as part of the Visual Arts Year, attracting 25,000 visitors.

The same year, **Gateshead Council** secures £800,000 funding for the **Angel of the North**.

Antony Gormley, *Field for the British Isles*, 1993. Photo courtesy Gateshead Council. Photo: Mark Pinder.

£584,000 from the National Lottery, £150,000 from the European Regional Development Fund, £45,000 from Northern Arts, as well as private sponsorship.

'Meanwhile Gateshead Council was angling for £38m from the National Lottery to convert the Baltic Flour Mills into the largest space for contemporary art outside London. The Arts Council announced the success of the bid in June 1997. Probably the Angel was a significant factor here – those who needed to be convinced were assured that Gateshead Council was serious in its partnership commitment to deliver contemporary art of international standard. Both [Jaume] Plensa's and Gormley's works have championed a £200m

July
Baltic Flour Mills, Towards the Vision
Following a research trip to various European galleries, Loveday Shewell and David Powell Associates publish a report outlining the early vision for the Baltic Flour Mills. With its emphasis on commissioning (rather than collecting) contemporary art, the report forms the basis for the Lottery application to the Arts Council the following year.

Les Levine, *See It Be It*, from *Public Pets*, Temporary Contemporary, 1996. Photo: Mark Pinder.

Temporary Contemporary: a series of visual art events on or around the Baltic Flour Mills, commissioned by Gateshead Council during the Visual Arts Year.

Participating artists: **Les Levine**,

Public Pets (Sep – Oct '96), curated by Declan McGonagle; **Diana Thater**, *Wicked Witch of the West* (Oct '96), curated by Iwona Blazwick; **Jaume Plensa**, *Blake in Gateshead* (Nov '96), curated by Sune Nordgren.

'Walking near the Tyne and thinking of Blake, I thought a new bridge was needed, a vertical bridge to bring us towards another kind of landscape. … To build a bridge, a bridge of light in Gateshead, near the Tyne and thinking of Blake.'
Jaume Plensa, 1996. Quoted in 'Temporary Contemporary' catalogue, Gateshead Council Libraries and Arts, 1996.

Defining Moments:
'In early May 1996 I attended my first meeting with Gateshead Council officers and the Baltic Design Team as Special Projects Adviser to the Council. My advice to that meeting – later adopted – was that two fundamental changes to the Design were needed even at that late stage. First, the Baltic project had to presuppose the existence of a bridge to the Newcastle Quayside and orient itself to the north rather than to the south. Secondly, the Baltic project

regeneration scheme for East Gateshead that is bringing an 80-hectare wasteland back to life.'
Mike White, former Assistant Director for Arts, Gateshead Council Libraries and Arts Dept., in *Making An Angel*, 1998. Both Mike White and the then Visual Arts Manager Anna Pepperall, were instrumental in the development of Gateshead's Public Art programme during the late 80s – 90s.

July
The Book of Hours
Twenty-four embroidered panels made by community groups and schools in Gateshead, each showing a different hour of the day. Made for the Visual Arts Year in 1996 and exhibited, in July, at the Shipley Art Gallery.

A new entrance to the **Laing Art Gallery**, Newcastle, is opened, funded by the Foundation for Sport and the Arts, the European Regional Development Fund and Newcastle City Council.

Richard Wilson, *The Joint's Jumping*
Unrealised proposal for neon artwork, designed by artist Richard Wilson, for the exterior of the Baltic Flour Mills, curated by Locus+.

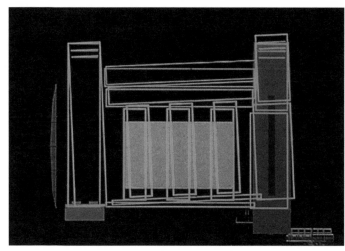

Richard Wilson, *The Joint's Jumping*, 1996. Computer generated image/proposal for BALTIC, the Centre for Contemporary Art, Gateshead. © Richard Wilson. Image credit: Interactive Architecture Ltd.

had to capitalise on its location at the bridgehead by creating a bar/retail complex in a new building on that site. With these two actions it was possible to project sufficient visitor numbers and trading income to construct a believable Lottery application.

On 19 March 1997 I led the Baltic team during the main assessment visit by an Arts Council team led by Adrian Ellis. At 6.00 p.m. – after a solid 10 hours of detailed questioning – both sides took a break on the open deck of the Pitcher and Piano. After half an hour a heavy rain squall came down the Tyne Gorge and everyone went inside. As the squall cleared, the sun came out and we had a perfect rainbow. From our vantage point the rainbow ended in the top of the Baltic. It seemed the gods were smiling.'
Peter Stark, Director of the Centre for Cultural Policy and Management at the University of Newcastle, 2002.

Bill Viola, *The Messenger*, 1996. Commissioned by The Chaplaincy to the Arts and Recreation in North East England for Durham Cathedral. Photo: Keera Perov.

The West Wind, a sculpture by **Laurent Reynes** consisting of forty iron girders decorated with cobalt blue ceramic tiles, installed at Kibblesworth, Gateshead, as part of the **Year of Visual Arts**.

September
Bill Viola's *The Messenger* Installed at Durham Cathedral during Visual Arts Year. Commissioned by the Chaplaincy to the Arts and Recreation in North East England.

November
Two **ceramic murals** (*Across Two Cultures* and *Bridges of Friendship*) are sited at Gateshead

Leisure Centre and Gateshead Central Library. The murals, designed by local and Japanese potters with tiles made by members of the public at Bensham Pottery, are the culmination of the **Komatsu Artists' Exchange Programme**, established in 1994.

1996

Gateshead Council lodges its application with the Arts Council of England for capital funds and revenue support for the conversion of the Baltic Flour Mills into a centre for contemporary art.

Defining Moment:
6 November 1996:
'I hired a car in Newcastle and drove the completed application – 19 boxes of documents – for the Baltic Flour Mills to London arriving at two in the morning. At that time I was Vice Chair of London Arts Board, and at eight the next morning I had a breakfast meeting with Mary Allen (then Secretary General of the Arts Council) and Prof. Christopher Frayling (RCA and member of ACE) to choose Trevor Phillips as the new chair of LAB. I gave Mary and Christopher a lift to the Arts Council in the car: only just enough room for the Secretary General and the Baltic on the back seat of the car. Christopher and Moss Cooper helped me unload the application, which filled the Arts Council's foyer.'
David Powell, David Powell Associates Ltd.

16 November – 9 February '97
'Serious Games', Laing Art Gallery, Newcastle; Barbican Art Gallery, London, June – August 1997.

An exhibition of contemporary interactive art, curated by Beryl Graham.
Includes work by artists Diller + Scofidio, Ritsuko Taho, Char Davies, Ann Whitehurst, Toshio Iwai, Bill Seaman, Harwood & Jim Campbell.

15–17 November
Digital Dreams 4, Newcastle
Fourth annual art and technology conference (initiated by Northern Arts in 1992; held every year until 1996) organised by Lisa Haskell

and Helen Sloane to coincide with the exhibition 'Serious Games'.

New Writing North
Established in 1996 as the writing development agency for the Northern Arts region. NWN exists to identify and develop new writing talent, to strengthen the writing economy in the region and to develop audiences and new contexts for literature. New Writing North also manages the Northern Writers' Awards and the Northern Rock Foundation Writer Award.
www.newwritingnorth.com

Our Friends in the North
broadcast on BBCTV.

Drama series following four Tyneside friends from the early '60s to the mid '90s. Written by Peter Flannery and with a cast that includes Christopher Ecclestone, Gina McKee and Daniel Craig.

June
The **Fine Art Department** at the University of Newcastle mounts a vigorous campaign to save the **Hatton Gallery**, which is threatened with closure.

A donation from **Dame Catherine Cookson** (1906 – 98) helps to ensure the future of the gallery as an exhibition venue and a valuable resource for students.

David Mach's brick sculpture, *Train*, is unveiled in Darlington on 23 June.
Commissioned by Morrison Supermarkets PLC and Darlington Borough Council (as part of Darlington's contribution to the

November
Jaume Plensa's light beam sculpture *Blake in Gateshead* is lit for the first time outside the Baltic Flour Mills.

Jaume Plensa, *Blake in Gateshead*, 1996.
Photo: Stephen Collins.

Visual Arts UK 1996), the sculpture is an actual-size representation of a 1930s steam locomotive emerging from a tunnel. Made from over 180,000 house bricks and costing £760,000 in total, the sculpture is the source of some criticism in the local press, despite using a local workforce in its construction. See Usherwood, Beach and Morris, *Public Sculpture in the North East of England*, pp.240–241.

July
VANE97 (Visual Arts North East) The first ever VANE festival is initiated by an informal grouping of artists and consists of the work of almost fifty artists in thirteen exhibitions and events.

Gateshead Libraries and Arts Service is awarded the £10,000 first prize in the Japan Festival Awards for the Komatsu Artists' Exchange project.

October – November
VANE98 (Visual Arts North East) The second VANE event comprises almost fifty exhibitions featuring the work of over 150 artists spread throughout the city of Newcastle, with projects also presented in Gateshead and North and South Tyneside. Venues include churches, cafés and restaurants, a Metro station, a railway tunnel, hospitals, empty offices and a library. The event is supported by BALTIC.

May – August
artranspennine98
An exhibition of international contemporary visual art in thirty different locations across the transpennine region of the UK,

initiated by Lewis Biggs and Robert Hopper.
Includes the Locus+ commission, Anya Gallaccio's *Two Sisters*, in the Minerva Basin, Hull.

February
The *Angel of the North* by **Antony Gormley** is installed in Gateshead.

Commissioned by Gateshead Council (whose 'Art in Public Places' Panel actually coined its now-famous title), the controversial public sculpture is 20m high, has a wingspan of 54m and is made from 200 tonnes of Cor-Ten steel. The sculpture's body and wings are transported, overnight, on trucks

June
The Arts Council awards £33.4m from the National Lottery for the conversion of the **Baltic Flour Mills** into an international arts venue, plus a further £1.5m a year revenue funding for the first five years post-opening. The award is celebrated with a press call from the roof of the Baltic Flour Mills.

Lithuanian sound and video artists visit and make work about the Baltic Flour Mills as part of a collaboration between Gateshead Libraries and Arts, Beaconsfield, London and the University of Sunderland.

Sune Nordgren in front of BALTIC, 1999.
Photo: Ulla Montan, 1999.

November
Sune Nordgren appointed director of BALTIC.
Sune Nordgren and Dominic Williams immediately begin working together on the redesign of the BALTIC building, a process that continues until May 1998.

from Hartlepool on 14 February and the work installed on its hillside site the following day. Now one of the most viewed public artworks in Britain, the *Angel* is visited by an estimated 150,000 people a year and is the most recent addition to Gateshead Council's public art programme.
(Inaugurated 16 February, unveiled 20 June)
For the full story of the making of the *Angel of the North*, see *Making an Angel*, Booth-Clibborn Editions, 1998.

'A flour mill provides material for the sustenance of the body. Now this great block of brick at the river's edge will become a resonating chamber in which new forms of art engage the mind.'

Antony Gormley, quoted in Gateshead Council's overview document, Baltic Flour Mills, 1997.

'Gateshead Council's Libraries and Arts team has, over the last fifteen years, established a track record for innovative programmes in the Visual Arts, and a dedicated approach to Public Art and artists working in social contexts. We have taken the audience and artists with us, from the earliest residencies to the "Angel of the North". We hope they will now enjoy and benefit from the manifestation of our past programme in the exciting new climate and context of BALTIC and its unfolding programme.'
Anna Pepperall, Public Art Curator, Gateshead Council, 2002.

Antony Gormley, *Angel of the North*, 1998.
Photo: Doug Hall, image courtesy of Gateshead Council.

Artist **Julian Opie** engaged as partner in BALTIC design team.

Julian Opie, drawing, 1998 © Julian Opie

Establishment of the first **BALTIC Trust**, with Sandy Nairne as Convenor (until January 1999).

July – October '99
Natalie Frost appointed as first Artist-in-Residence, as part of BALTIC pre-opening programme (in collaboration with Gateshead Council Libraries and Arts and funded by the Paul Hamlyn Foundation). She is based in a studio in Gateshead Town Centre.

Defining Moments:
'The ability, confidence and eager-ness of a group of pensioners from the Old Ford to take on alien and complex ideas, led me to believe that the enjoyment of contemporary art need not be exclusive in terms of class and education.'
Natalie Frost, BALTIC Artist-in-Residence, July '98 – October '99.

Next page: Jaume Plensa, *Blake in Gateshead*, 1996. Photo: Stephen Collins.

May
Northern Architecture (formerly Northern Architecture Centre Ltd.) becomes operational, with the appointment of Mark Daniels as Programme Director. Northern Architecture seeks to raise awareness and understanding of architecture and the built environment across the North of England.
www.north.org.uk

Northern Arts initiates its '**Study and Stay**' programme, to develop different ways of supporting graduates from the northern region.

The first year's scheme sees five artists graduating from BA courses in the region placed with different studios, and results in an exhibition at the Hatton Gallery. The following year of this strategic programme involves MA students and culminates in a show at NGCA in Sunderland. In 2000, twenty artists are given small bursaries to make work for that year's VANE festival whilst the current scheme sees artists placed in creative industries in the region.

23 October
The **National Glass Centre** (designed by Gollifer Associates) opens in Sunderland. The Centre, the first major building to open in the UK funded by a Capital Arts Lottery award, is devoted to the science, the production and the art of glass.

The **Arc** in Stockton-on-Tees opens. The £6.5m centre for the arts includes a permanent commission from artist Richard Wilson (*Over Easy*), in which a section of the building's façade continually revolves.

November – January '99
New Contemporaries – the annual exhibition of work by recent fine art graduates in the UK – is shown at the Hatton Gallery, Newcastle.

September – October '99
David Goard appointed as Artist-in-Residence.

The **Kittiwake Tower** is erected at the Baltic Flour Mills site and that summer over 100 birds are nesting on it. In March 2001, the structure is successfully relocated to Saltmeadows, half a mile downstream from BALTIC on the banks of the Tyne, and within a few weeks, 100 pairs of birds have moved onto the tower in its new location.

An adult kittiwake.

Kittiwakes nesting on the tower.
Photo: Peter Bell.

Cover page, BALTIC Newsletter No.1.

November
BALTIC Newsletter No.1 published.
Contents: Etienne Clément's photo-portraits of BALTIC; project background; B4B information.

2 – 3 November
Two **Reunion Evenings** are held at The Shipley Art Gallery in Gateshead for former workers of the Baltic Flour Mills. Over forty people participate, their recollections, photographs and other artifacts forming the basis for the **Baltic Memories** exhibition and documentary film.

December – June 1999
Commencement of the 'enabling works'. This involves the removal of 148 grain silos inside the building. When the enabling works finish (in June 1999) only the north and south brick facades of the building remain, held in place by an intricate scaffolding cage.

8 December
Bridge: temporary installation by BALTIC Artist-in-Residence **David Goard** in Gateshead town centre.

Enabling works in progress.
Photo: Department of Architectural Services, Gateshead Council.

January
Appointment of **Alan J. Smith** as Chairman of the BALTIC Trust.

February 1999
BALTIC Newsletter No.2
Contents: B4B update and BALTIC floor plans

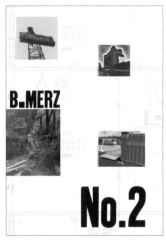

Cover page, BALTIC Newsletter No.2.

July
As part of **Art on the Riverside**, the largest programme of public art in the UK, two new sculptures are installed on Tyneside:

Tyne Anew, by American artist **Mark di Suvero**, is installed by the docks in North Shields. The 21-metre high iron structure is inspired by the North East's industrial heritage and reflects the dockyard setting.

1999

March – April
VANE Export, Tensta Konsthall, Stockholm
A collaboration with Waygood Gallery, Newcastle
(Artists: Rupert Clamp; Jo Coupe; Jennifer Douglas; Antoinette Hächler; Helen Smith; Matt Stokes; Paul Stone)

Waygood Boutique at Tensta Konsthall, Sweden, as part of 'VANE Export', 1999. Photo: Lynne Otter, 1999.

Before the opening in the autumn 2001, BALTIC will run an advanced program with international exhibitions, events & seminars outside

No.3

Cover page, BALTIC Newsletter No.3.

March
BALTIC Newsletter No.3
B4B statement; Anish Kapoor; Kurt Schwitters; 'FLASH' DVD; Baltic Memories; Paul Hamlyn Foundation

16 April – 22 May
'No Socks', Kurt Schwitters and the *MerzBarn*
Hatton Gallery, The University of Newcastle

An exhibition of the German avant-garde artist, focusing on work produced during his last years in the Lake District. The exhibition, a collaboration with the Hatton Gallery at the University of Newcastle and the Sprengel Museum in Hanover, is organised to celebrate the renovation of Schwitters' famous *MerzBarn* installation, permanently installed in the Hatton Gallery.

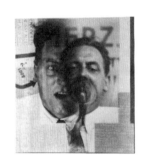

No.4

Cover page, BALTIC Newsletter No.4. showing Kurt Schwitters, photo by El Lissitzky, 1924. Reproduced by kind permission of Sprengel Museum Hannover, © VG Bild-Kunst, Germany.

April
BALTIC Newsletter No.4
Special issue to accompany the Kurt Schwitters exhibition at the

Conversation Piece by **Juan Muñoz**, consisting of twenty-two life-size bronze figures, is permanently installed at the mouth of the Tyne in South Shields. (Originally commissioned for IMMA, Dublin, another version of the piece was previously shown in Berwick-upon-Tweed as part of the celebrations for the 1996 Visual Arts Year.)

Juan Muñoz, *Conversation Piece*, 1996. Photo: Attilio Maranzano.

Hatton Gallery, Newcastle, containing texts by Per Kirkeby, Karin Orchard and Sarah Wilson.

Baltic Memories' exhibition leaflet.

1 May – 13 June
'Baltic Memories'
Shipley Art Gallery, Gateshead
An exhibition of recollections, personal histories and artifacts from people who worked in and around the Baltic Flour Mills. A collaboration with Gateshead Council, Libraries and Arts and Tyne and Wear Museums. The exhibition is accompanied by a documentary film by A19 Film and Video including interviews with former employees of the flour mill.

June
End of enabling works.

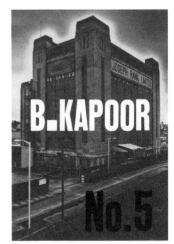

Cover page, BALTIC Newsletter No.3.

June
BALTIC Newsletter No.5
Contents: B.KAPOOR: a site-specific installation at BALTIC by Anish Kapoor; Sune Nordgren and Anish Kapoor in conversation; *TARATANTARA* sketches and technical drawings; Anish Kapoor CV; B4B update.

7 July – 1 September
Anish Kapoor, *TARATANTARA*
BALTIC, Gateshead
A site-specific installation by Anish Kapoor, commissioned specially for BALTIC before the construction of the new building begins. Over 50m long and 25m wide, the work is in-situ for eight weeks and is seen by over 16,000 people. (Shown in 2000 in Naples, Italy)

'…a landmark in contemporary art… a monumental masterwork.'
Richard Cork, *The Times*, 1 September

'I liked this wonderful possibility of working in a space of these dimensions. How often does one work in a space that is 45m high, 51m long and 25m wide as a shell, a single form? There is a great energy in it.'
Anish Kapoor, from an interview with Sune Nordgren, May '99, printed in BALTIC Newsletter No.5.

Anish Kapoor, *TARATANTARA*, 1999. Photo: John Riddy © John Riddy

September
The £9m **Centre for Visual Arts in Cardiff** opens in the city's Old Library.

Ambit by **Alison Wilding** is installed in the River Wear on the site of the former Austin's shipyard. Part of the Art on the Riverside programme, the 20m steel sculpture, which describes the outline of a ship, changes its shape with the variable conditions of the river and is illuminated at night.

September – November
The **1st Liverpool Biennial of international contemporary art** (including the exhibition

'TRACE'; John Moores 21; New Contemporaries 99 and 'Tracey').

October – November
VANE99
The 3rd VANE features over eighty exhibitions and events, with almost 200 artists taking part. (Includes 'Tongue 'n Groove': an exhibition curated by Artist-in-Residence Natalie Frost in empty shop unit in Gateshead High Street.)

'Tongue 'n Groove', installation shot, showing wallpaper piece by Natalie Frost.

Anish Kapoor, *TARATANTARA*, 1999. Photo: Ravi Deepres

Defining moments:
'*The black and white BALTIC flag fluttering piratically over the gutted building, whilst in the void beneath, the stretched red material of*

Kapoor's TARATANTARA quivered slightly like some enormous life form taking up residence.'
Richard Deacon, artist and BALTIC Trustee, April 2002.

7 July
Anish Kapoor is the first recipient of a 'Joseph': a cast-iron model of the BALTIC building in miniature produced at Hargreaves Foundry in Halifax and presented to each artist who is commissioned by BALTIC.

The Joseph. Photo: Phil Snow, Dept. Architectural Services, Gateshead Council.

September
Construction of new building begins.
(Contractors: HBG Construction Ltd)

September
FLASH DVD
A collaboration with Bifrons Foundation, Amsterdam

A series of nine DVD's, produced by visual artists and contemporary composers. The series is premiered at the World Wide Video festival at the Stedilijk Museum, Amsterdam in September '99:

Composers & Artists
Maarten Altena & Ger van Elk

Louis Andriessen & Marijke van Warmerdam

Erik Calmes & Henk Peeters

Roderik de Man & Maura Biava

Chiel Meijering & Jaap Kroneman

BALTIC staff, September 1999.
Left to right: Sune Nordgren, Viki Lewis, Anne Howes, Sarah Martin,
Stephen Cleland and Jo Wilson. Photo: Keith Paisley.

Artists **Jane and Louise Wilson** are nominated for the **Turner Prize**.
(awarded to Steve McQueen)

3 December – 15 January
Susan Hiller, *Psi Girls* screened at NGCA.

1 January – 31 December
The **New Millennium Experience** opens at the Millennium Dome in Greenwich, London. Includes artworks by Richard Deacon, Antony Gormley and Anish Kapoor.

2000

Maura Biava, still from *For Uranus*, 1999.

Maarten van Norden & Annette Messenger

Paul Termos & Ansuya Blom

Vodershow & Liza May Post

Martijn Padding & Jean-Claude Ruggirello

Cover page, BALTIC Newsletter No.6, drawing by Grennan and Sperandio

October
BALTIC Newsletter No.6
Contents: Grennan and Sperandio; BALTIC Professor of Contemporary Art, Susan Hiller; FLASH DVD; Newcastle and Gateshead aerial drawing; *TARATANTARA* images by Etienne Clément; BALTIC staff

Vicki Lewis joins BALTIC as Curator.

January – January 03
Susan Hiller is appointed BALTIC Professor of Contemporary Art at the University of Newcastle.

What are you most looking forward to about BALTIC?
'Outstanding art in a beautiful building, and the smell of bread!'
Susan Hiller, 2002.

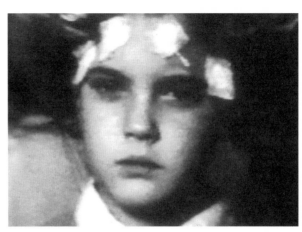

Susan Hiller, still from *Psi Girls*, 1999.

6 January
Newcastle Arts Centre re-opens after an extensive upgrade, including a full-time gallery and an art materials store.

16 February
Opening of **The New Art Gallery**, Walsall, designed by architects Caruso St. John.

The New Art Gallery, Walsall.
Photo: Helene Binet.

28–30 April
live-stock, Arc, Stockton-on-Tees
(includes screening of FLASH DVD project)

live-stock ram/fm was a 72-hour experimental audio event, transmitted live on local fm and webcast via the internet from Arc, Stockton-on-Tees. Showcasing live performances, workshops and presentations, the project avoided traditional radio formats and brought together a wide range of material and international participants, including artists, writers, djs, musicians, media centres and community groups.

Initiated by Kate Rich during her residency at Arc, the project

Francis Gomila, *Millennium Chicken*, 2000. Proposal for feeding the public by transforming an ordinary cargo container into a touring, spit-roasting sculptural installation, capable of roasting 144 chickens in one single performance.

January – December
Francis Gomila, BALTIC Artist-in-Residence, based at AiR Space, Gateshead town centre.

February – February 03
Sarah Cook is appointed PhD Research Student in New Media Curating at the University of Sunderland, in collaboration with BALTIC.

February
BALTIC Newsletter No.7
Contents: 'New Sites – New Art, the first BALTIC International Seminar; 'To Collect or not to Collect? That is the Question'; Artist-in-Residence; B4B re-cap; BALTIC: The Story so Far)

Cover page, BALTIC Newsletter No.7.

30 March
The Producers: Contemporary Curators in Conversation
A series of discussions initiated by Susan Hiller, Vicki Lewis and Andrew Burton at the University of Newcastle.

The first event in the series sees **James Lingwood** and **Sune Nordgren** in conversation.

'BALTIC and the new Tate both see themselves as producing organisations, as does Artangel. The transformation from a more passive mode of housing art, to a more active mode of producing (art works and meanings) has quickened in the last few years within an international economy which is increasingly competitive.'
James Lingwood, *The Producers*, June 2000.

included live performances by Project Dark, zoviet*france, Salad Butty and A String Thing, Serafuse, Moneyshot and Jazzfinger, artist presentations by Hayley Newman and Mongrel, a video programme, a poetry slam and a tea-dance. There were over 70 contributors; for a full list, visit the archive at: www.live-stock.org.

28 April
The Lowry Centre, designed by Michael Wilford & Partners, opens in Salford Quays, Manchester.

12 May
Tate Modern opens in the former Bankside Power Station, London. Designed by architects Herzog & de Meuron, the gallery is home to the Tate collection of international modern and contemporary art, displayed thematically in over eighty new gallery spaces. Collection display includes Susan Hiller's mixed-media installation *From the Freud Museum (1991–96)*.

The first in the Unilever Series of annual commissions for Tate Modern's Turbine Hall is awarded to sculptor Louise Bourgeois.

Tate Modern, Exterior – Northside.
© Tate Photography.

7 – 9 April
New Sites-New Art, 1st BALTIC International Seminar, St. Mary's Church, Gateshead
Speakers: Tuula Arkio, Kiasma Museum of Contemporary Art, Helsinki; Jan Debbaut, Stedlijk van Abbemuseum, Eindhoven; David Elliott, Moderna Museet, Stockholm; Peter Jenkinson, New Art Gallery, Walsall; András Pálffy & Christian Jabornegg, architects; Dominic Williams, architect.

What are you most looking forward to about BALTIC?
'The results and fruits of the concept which is based on a strong co-operation between the artist and the institution, creating something new together instead of just showing things from the past. It will show that important work for contemporary art can also be done outside the "centres". The geographical location is not the issue. It is

the ambition and creativity that makes all the difference.'
Tuula Arkio, Director General, Finnish National Galleries

St Mary's Church, Gateshead.
Photo: Phil Snow, Dept Architectural Services, Gateshead Council.

18 April
Gateshead Quays Visitor Centre (and offices for BALTIC and Music Centre, Gateshead) officially opens at St. Mary's Church, one of Gateshead's oldest buildings, dating from the 14th century.
The £250m Gateshead Quays development includes BALTIC, the Music Centre Gateshead, Gateshead Millennium Bridge and BALTIC Square, to form one of the most ambitious new arts, culture and leisure developments in Europe.

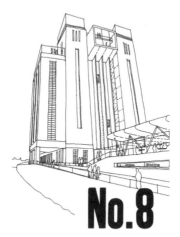

Cover page, BALTIC Newsletter No.8.

BALTIC Newsletter No.8
Contents: Architectural drawings by Dominic Williams; Excerpts from 'New Sites – New Art' seminar,

Susan Hiller,
Witness, 2000.
Image: courtesy
of the artist.

16 May – 25 June
Susan Hiller's audio-installation *Witness* is shown for the first time at The Chapel, Golborne Road, London. (The piece is also shown later that year in the exhibition, 'Intelligence: New British Art 2000', Tate Britain, London, 6 June – 24 September 2000, and at the Havana Biennial, November – December 2000.)

May – September
The Sitooteries, Belsay Hall Castle and Gardens, Northumberland. Twelve temporary outdoor structures commissioned from artists, architects and designers including Julian Opie, Tanya Kovats and FAT.

Rest Area, 2000, Julian Opie.
Photo: Keith Paisley.

Co-organised by English Heritage (as part of the Year of Public Sculpture) Northern Arts and Northern Architecture.

June 2000 – May 2001
Year of the Artist
A year-long, national project, part of the Millennium Festival for the Year 2000 and the culmination of the Arts Council's Arts 2000 series (begun in 1992) celebrating different art forms in different parts of the country. Year of the Artist aims to celebrate artists and promote greater awareness of the role and status of the arts through the support of 1000 artists' residencies in the UK.

October
Billy Elliot released. Directed by Stephen Daldry, starring Jamie Bell and Julie Walters and filmed in County Durham during 1999.

Year of the Artist
Residencies with Nexus
Nexus, in partnership with New Writing North, host a series of residencies for audio writer Carol McGuigan, artist Topsy Qur'et and poet Subhadassi, who work with Metro staff and passengers to develop a series of temporary events around the system.

Culminates in a live event involving 100 people and organised by Topsy Qur'et at Gateshead Metro Station on the night of Friday 13 October. The event is filmed and the resulting video, *Goatsheadloop*, is screened in a Metro ticket machine at Gateshead during November–December 2000.

2000

8 June
The Producers:
Matthew Higgs and **Clive Philpott** in conversation, University of Newcastle.

Francis Gomila, still from *The Fall*, single channel video, 15 mins, 2000
© Francis Gomila

10 June
Goodbye Alf Roberts: Talk by **Owen Luder**, architect of Gateshead Car Park, in the top-floor restaurant space of the car park.

(Organised by Artist-in-Residence Francis Gomila as part of *Architecture Week*, in collaboration with Northern Architecture.)

22 June
Screening of **FLASH DVD**'s at the Whitechapel Gallery, London.

Martín Weber, from 'Dream Series': *Love*, 1992.

11 July – 3 September
Martín Weber, photographs from the 'Dream Series', Side Gallery, Newcastle.

16 June
Artist **Bill Viola** is awarded
an Honorary Degree from the
University of Sunderland.

June
The **Big M**, a portable venue
for video and digital media work
created by Isis Arts and designers
Inflate, is launched at the Centre
for Life, Newcastle. For its inaugural tour, the *Big M* presents
21 newly-commissioned and
contemporary works by 16 artists
including Cecile Babiole, Bureau
of Inverse Technology and
Veronique Chance.
See www.isisarts.org.uk for details of
2002–2003 Big M tour

The *Big M* launch, Newcastle, June 2000.
An Isis Arts New Media Production. Photo: Stan Gamester.

22 July – 26 August 2000
NEO (North East Open)
Waygood Gallery, Newcastle;
Globe Gallery, South Shields.

11 September
Kielder Skyspace, by American
artist **James Turrell**, opens in
Kielder Forest, Northumberland.
The first circular Skyspace to be
constructed in the world, *Kielder
Skyspace* is a cylindrical chamber
built into the rock, the open roof of
which makes the changing light
conditions of the sky above visible.

Clock melted by fire at St. Mary's
Church, September 2000.

6 September
BALTIC Offices, St Mary's
Church, damaged in a fire.

Cover page, BALTIC Newsletter No.9.

September
BALTIC Newsletter No.9
published
Contents: B.INSIDE: A guide to the
interior spaces and resources at BALTIC;
B4B update.

1 October
BALTIC and **Waygood Gallery**
representatives take part in relay
over the Swing Bridge, Newcastle.
(As part of a project by artist
Veronique Chance for the exhibition

'We Interrupt this programme',
Waygood Gallery, Newcastle,
October – November 2000)
BALTIC team: Hannah Barnes,
Angela Hedley, Vicki Lewis,
Sarah Martin.

BALTIC and Waygood running teams, 1 October 2000.
Top row: Sarah Martin, Angela Hedley, Hannah Barnes, Vicki Lewis.
Bottom row: Helen Smith, Gordon Dalton, Veronique Chance, Gillian Nicol, Chris Yeats.

James Turrell, *Kielder Skyspace*, 2000.
Photo: Mark Pinder.

September
Newcastle-based singer-songwriter
Kathryn Williams is nominated
for the Mercury Music Prize this
year.
Williams' debut album, *Dog Leap
Stairs* is released in 1999, followed,
in 2000, by *Little Black Numbers*.

30 September – 10 November
**LMN (Liverpool, Manchester,
Newcastle)**
A series of three exhibitions in
which artist-curators involved in
the exhibitions Tracey (Liverpool),
MART99 (Manchester) and VANE
(Newcastle) select work to be

Cover page, BALTIC Newsletter No.10.

October
BALTIC Newsletter No.10
Special edition designed by Jenny Holzer

B.READ/ONE & TWO.

October
Publication of **B.READ/ONE**,
Artists at Work and
B.READ/TWO, *The Producers*.

exhibited in the curators' home cities. The Newcastle strand, *Inferno*, takes place from 14 October – 10 November at The Guildhall and is curated by Paul Stone.

October – November
VANE2000
The 4th and final VANE event features over eighty exhibitions and the work of almost 200 artists. The catalogue is supported by BALTIC.

7 November
The **Centre for Visual Arts in Cardiff** closes after just fourteen months in operation.

The new **Millennium Bridge** arrives in Gateshead. The 850-tonne suspension bridge is carried, in one piece, by crane from the AMEC yard in Wallsend where it was constructed, before being delicately lowered into place over the River Tyne. Months of testing follow, and the Bridge is opened to the public in September 2001.

Gateshead Millennium Bridge, November 2001.

19 October
The Producers:
Gilane Tawadros and **Hans Ulrich Obrist** in conversation.

25 – 28 October
Jenny Holzer, Xenon projections
BALTIC, Gateshead,
Tuxedo Princess and The Castle Keep, Newcastle

A series of text projections over four nights onto the façades of three prominent public sites in Newcastle and Gateshead: the Castle Keep, the Tuxedo Princess boat/nightclub and BALTIC. The sites, selected for the location, their history or their function, serve as dramatic backdrops for Holzer's powerful, arresting and poetic texts.

In conjunction with the Xenon text projections, a selection of Holzer's one-line *Truisms* are printed onto thousands of beer mats, which are distributed throughout the region.

For this project, the first large presentation of her work in the UK for over a decade, Jenny Holzer also designs a special edition of the BALTIC Newsletter (No.10).

Jenny Holzer, from *Lamentz*. Xenon projection onto BALTIC, Gateshead, October 25, 2000.
Photo: Attilio Maranzano. Courtesy Cheim and Read, New York. © Jenny Holzer.

Right: Jenny Holzer, from *Truisms*, BALTIC, Gateshead, October 25, 2000.
Photo: Attilio Maranzano. Courtesy Cheim and Read, New York. © Jenny Holzer.

December
Anish Kapoor, *TARATANTARA*, installed in the Piazza Plebiscito, Naples.

5 December
BALTIC Professor of Contemporary Art **Susan Hiller**, Lectures at The University of Newcastle.

Anish Kapoor, *TARATANTARA*, in Naples, 2000.
Photo: Jasper Sharp.

25 October
Joseph No.2 awarded to Jenny Holzer.

26 – 28 October
Artists at Work, 2nd BALTIC International Seminar
Speakers: Daniel Birnbaum, IASPIS, Stockholm; Lynne Cooke, Dia Center for the Arts, New York; Kathryn Kanjo, ArtPace, San Antonio; Friedrich Meschede, DAAD, Berlin; Richard Wentworth, artist.

'I think residency programmes can, if they work well, represent a positive counter-movement to the global levelling that is happening more and more now in the art world. It's about creating a connection to one place, to a local audience and maybe a local tradition and history.'
Daniel Birnbaum, *Artists at Work*, October 2001.

30 October – 13 November
Domestic Installation, photographs by pupils from Joseph Swann School working with Francis Gomila, BALTIC Artist-in-Residence, as part of a child safety project in Gateshead.

Cover page, BALTIC Newsletter No.11.

November
BALTIC Newsletter No.11
Contents: Marijke van Warmerdam, *Weather forecast*; Jenny Holzer in conversation with Sune Nordgren; photographs of Jenny Holzer projections on Tyneside; B4B update; A History of the Future programme details.

23 November
The Producers:
Charles Esche and **Frances Morris**

'It's interesting to be called a "producer" in this context because I think there is a shortage of vocabulary for the sorts of things we're doing now. There are very few nominal roles you can get involved with if you're dealing with art: artist, critic, curator and then you start to run out of terms. That's something of a disadvantage because as curators or artists we are all working in rather different ways and with different objectives.'
Charles Esche, *The Producers*, November 2001.

7 December
The Producers:
Guy Brett and **Deanna Petherbridge** in conversation.

7–31 December
Marijke van Warmerdam,
Weather forecast
Grey Street, Newcastle
Weather forecast is a 35mm film
loop by Marijke van Warmerdam
commissioned by BALTIC and
premiered in Newcastle.

Repetition is a recurring theme
in Marijke van Warmerdam's film
loops, in which simple activities are
repeated to mesmerising effect.
In *Weather forecast* a range of
climatic conditions occur one after
another in a single take. At the
centre of the film a persistently
overflowing bathtub represents
the continuity of life against the
backdrop of the ever-changing
weather, which remains a constant
source of fascination for us all.
From BALTIC Newsletter No.11,
November 2000.

7 December
Joseph No.3 awarded to Marijke
van Warmerdam.

BALTIC staff, December 2000. Left to right: Vicki Lewis, Hannah Barnes, Jo Wilson,
Sarah Martin, Angela Hedley, Sune Nordgren, Stephen Cleland, Emma Thomas and
Anne Howes. Photo: Keith Paisley.

Marijke van Warmerdam, *Weather forecast*, 35mm film loop, Newcastle, 2000.
Courtesy Galerie Riis, Oslo. Photo: Keith Paisley, 2000. © Marijke van Warmerdam

Marijke van Warmerdam, still from *Weather forecast*, 2000. © Marijke van Warmerdam

March
Government announces abolition of entrance fees to national museums and galleries in England (to come into effect later in the year).

April – June
'**Nothing**', an exhibition curated by Ele Carpenter and Graham Gussin, at NGCA (Northern Gallery for Contemporary Art), Sunderland.

The exhibition and accompanying publication explore ideas around the notion of 'nothing' and include contributions from artists such as Francis Alÿs, Fiona Banner, Anya Gallaccio, Hans Haacke, Douglas Heubler, Robert Smithson, Catherine Yass and Andy Warhol. (Exhibition later tours to Contemporary Art Centre, Vilnius and Rooseum, Malmö.)

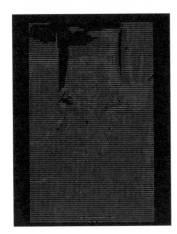

Vuk Cosic, 2000 © Vuk Cosic.

January
A History of the Future
(A Northern Architecture Project in collaboration with BALTIC, Globe Gallery, Waygood Gallery, Nexus and the Photographers' Gallery)

New Media Guest Curator Sarah Cook commissions BALTIC's first web commission – **Vuk Cosic**'s *www.thisistherealmatrix.com* – to coincide with the screening of the film *The Matrix* at Tyneside Cinema, Newcastle.

Tod Hanson's epic, futuristic vision of the Newcastle and Gateshead Quaysides (*Untitled*, 2000) is exhibited at Gateshead Quays Visitor Centre.

Tod Hanson, *Untitled*, 2000, iridescent acrylic on board, 4915 x 2458mm (detail). © Tod Hanson

22 February
The Producers:
Sharon Kivland and **Adam Szymczyk** in conversation, University of Newcastle.

March
BALTIC Newsletter No.12
Contents: 'Outlanders: Contemporary Artists from Stockholm'; B4B update; *TARATANTARA* in Naples; interview with Francis Gomila; building work in progress, November 2000. Photo: Etienne Clément.

8 March
The Producers:
Ralph Rugoff and **Richard Grayson** in conversation, University of Newcastle.

'I look back, in this very old-fashioned way, to the original meaning of the term "curate": the idea that a curator is someone who takes care of things. To me, the idea of taking care of a work

Cover page, BALTIC Newsletter No.12.

of art means to show it in a context where it's somehow going to be alive, to be allowed to do what it does well.'
Ralph Rugoff, *The Producers*, March 2001

15 March – 21 April
Outlanders
A collaboration with Waygood
Gallery, Newcastle, curated by
Sarah Martin and Paul Stone.
Artists: Charlotte Åberg; Thomas
Elovsson; Peter Geschwind; Felix
Gmelin; Thomas Karlsson; Gunilla
Klingberg; Lena Malm; Ebba Matz;
Jonas Nobel.

15 March
The Producers:
Jon Bewley and **Lisa Corrin**
in conversation
University of Newcastle

Outlanders: Contemporary Artists from Stockholm, Waygood Gallery, Newcastle, 2001.
Installation view showing work by Jonas Nobel, Lena Malm and Ebba Matz.
Photo: Colin Davison, 2001.

BALTIC

The Producers: Contemporary Curators in Conversation (2)

B.READ / FOUR

April
B.READ / FOUR
The Producers (2) published

Cover page, BALTIC Newsletter No.13.

March
BALTIC Newsletter No.13
Special issue: *The Hand and the Word*, designed by Grennan and Sperandio.

20–27 April
Grennan and Sperandio,
The Hand and the Word. Preview and week of screenings of animated film at The Little Theatre, Gateshead.

The Hand and the Word is a BALTIC commission involving a unique collaboration between artists Simon Grennan and Christopher Sperandio and the Progressive Players (Gateshead's longest-standing amateur dramatic society), who have worked together to produce a twenty-minute long animated film.

The script is taken from a short story written in 1827 by the Irish writer Gerald Griffin, now known as the world's first detective story. The animated film was developed collaboratively, beginning with the selection of Gerald Griffin's short story and its transformation into a script and a storyboard. The play was then staged at the Little Theatre in Gateshead as well as at sites on location. Grennan and Sperandio's process of turning the digital footage into over 4000 drawings for animation then followed. The end result is a film whose characters bear a close likeness to the actual actors.

Simon Grennan and Christopher Sperandio, from *The Hand and the Word*, 2001. © Grennan and Sperandio.

The Hand and the Word forms part of BALTIC's pre-opening programme B4B.
From BALTIC Newsletter No.13, April 2001.

May
Work starts on the site of the
Music Centre Gateshead
(due for completion in 2003).

Described as *'the pioneering
international centre for musical
discovery'* Northern Sinfonia and
Folkworks' new home is *'a spectacular Norman Foster building
on the south bank of the Tyne
alongside BALTIC. Its glazed
concourse enfolds working spaces
and concert halls of acoustic
excellence for music of all kinds
and a centre dedicated to achieving
a step-change in music education
across the region.'*

The Music Centre Gateshead, Foster and Partners.

20 April
Joseph's 4 & **5** awarded to
Simon Grennan and Christopher
Sperandio.

10–12 May
Curating New Media, **3rd BALTIC
International Seminar**
A collaboration with The University
of Sunderland/CRUMB
(Curatorial Research for Upstart
Media Bliss). Co-organised by
Sarah Cook and Beryl Graham.

Speakers: Tamas Banovich,
Postmasters Gallery, New York;
Sarah Cook, CRUMB; Vuk Cosic,
artist; Matthew Gansallo; Tate;
Karen Guthrie & Nina Pope, artists;
Iliyana Nedkova, FACT, Liverpool;
Julian Stallabrass, Courtauld
Institute, London; Thomson &
Craighead, artists; Mark Tribe,
rhizome.org, New York.

*'The museum brings to online artists
audiences that they otherwise might
find hard to reach, for it's easy to
languish in obscurity when the Web
is full of brash and rich commercial
sites and online artists clearly give
the museum a link into a rapidly
changing and alien culture. But
there is a real worry here I think,
that as other new media, like
photography and video for instance,
become accommodated by the
museum, many would say that
they changed too much in their
transformation into familiar-looking
works of art and the museum didn't
change enough. But the challenge
of online art is greater and it holds
out the hope for a transformation
of art in a democratic and participatory direction.'*
Julian Stallabrass, *Curating New Media*,
May 2001.

10 May
Joseph No.6 awarded to
Vuk Cosic.

Vuk Cosic with *Joseph*, May 2001.

15 May
The Hand and the Word is
screened on Tyne Tees Television.

June
TARATANTARA documentary by
A19 Film and Video screened at
Tate Modern as part of Architecture
Week.

Cover page, BALTIC Newsletter No.14.

June
BALTIC Newsletter No.14
Contents: 'B.In Venice', special issue for
the 2001 Venice Biennale: project background and presentation of the opening
commissions.

June – November
49th Venice Biennale. Artistic
Director: Harald Szeeman.
Britain is represented by Mark
Wallinger.

Vuk Cosic represents Slovenia
with his exhibition of net.art titled
'Temporary Autonomous Pavilion':
the first time a new media artist
has been recognised for networked
art within the national pavilions.

2001

5 – 9 June
Marijke van Warmerdam,
Weather forecast, Campo Santa
Margherita, Venice.
Commissioned by BALTIC and
shown during the 2001 Venice
Biennale.
(As part of the exhibition 'Post Nature',
Dutch Pavilion, Venice Biennale.)

20 June – 8 July
Janet Cardiff, *Forty Part Motet*,
Castle Keep, Newcastle.

A sound work by Janet Cardiff,
based on a piece of sacred
choral music, *Spem in alium*, by
sixteenth-century composer
Thomas Tallis. In *Forty Part Motet*,
forty separately recorded voices
are played back through speakers
placed strategically throughout
the space, allowing the audience
to experience the music from the
viewpoint of the singers.

Janet Cardiff,
Forty Part Motet,
2001.
Installation at
Castle Keep,
Newcastle, 2001.
Photo: Neville
Blaszk.

Commissioned by Field with the Arts
Council of England; Canada House;
The Salisbury Festival and the Salisbury

Cathedral Choir; BALTIC; The New Art
Gallery, Walsall; the NOW Festival
Nottingham.

20 June
Joseph No.7 awarded to Janet Cardiff.

20 June
Janet Cardiff talks about *Forty Part Motet* at the Castle Keep, Newcastle and gives a more detailed presentation about her work that evening at Gateshead Quays Visitor Centre.

'I see the artwork as a changeable sculpture. It is very much about the person's physical relationship to a space that has been permeated by sound. When you are walking around listening to the voices coming from the speakers, your path dictates how the music unfolds. Rather than the normal audience position of standing in front, letting the music mix to a unified whole, the activity of the people listening makes it so that every time a person hears it, it changes. Depending on your movement, you're hearing different elements of the composition, different combinations of the voices, so that in a way, the audience is very active in the piece, almost becoming a performer themselves.

We've installed it in three different spaces and every time it responds to the acoustics of the space in quite unique ways. Things like the way that the speakers are situated and the distance between them, also affect the sound.

One thing that I really like about the siting of Forty Part Motet *at the Castle Keep is that when you're walking up the stairs, the voices project out from the different alcoves. When you're standing on the stairs below, you can hear the sound as though it was a physical thing sitting on the steps waiting for you to go up and grab it. As you climb the stairs, the sound responds with the space of the structure and the echoes you hear create an environment that plays on the historical setting. Everything you hear is affected by the music.'*
Janet Cardiff, June 2001

BALTIC

Artists at Work

B.READ / THREE

July
Publication of B.READ/ THREE, *Artists at Work.*

173

September – November
'New Contemporaries' is
shown at NGCA, Sunderland.

15 September
BBC Proms in the Park is
broadcast live from Gateshead.
The first event in Gateshead's new
Baltic Square and one of the
inaugural events of the Music
Centre Gateshead, the concert
(which includes performances from
Kathryn Tickell and Northern
Sinfonia) is the centrepiece of
a weekend of live music events
on the square. Organised by
musicnorth in associaton with
Gateshead Council. (Other Proms
in the Park events take place in
London, Cornwall and Liverpool.)

Gateshead Millennium Bridge.
Photo: Graeme Peacock.
Image reproduced by kind
permission of Gateshead Council.

Cover and inside page, BALTIC Newsletter No.15

September
BALTIC Newsletter No.15
'BALTIC?'
Conceived by Alec Finlay, BALTIC visiting
artist, and produced in collaboration with
schools in the Borough of Gateshead.

24 October
The Producers:
Carolyn Christov-Bakargiev
and **Liam Gillick** in conversation
University of Newcastle.
*'A show by an artist can never
be as good as a really good show
by a curator, but it's always more
productive than a bad show by a
curator.'*
Liam Gillick, *The Producers*.

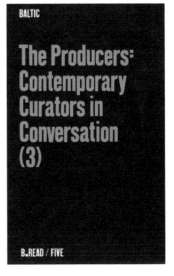

B.READ/FIVE, *The Producers* (3).

Northern Sinfonia and Folkworks give up independent status and merge into the North Music Trust, who will manage and programme the Music Centre Gateshead.

17 September
Gateshead Millennium Bridge opens to the public. Designed by Wilkinson Ere Architects/Gifford & Partners, the pedestrian and cycle bridge is the world's first to use a tilting mechanism in order to open.

13 – 14 October
Team Build weekend Organised by Anna Best in association with B + B, BALTIC and [a-n].

1 November
The new **Centenary Development** at Tate Britain is opened to the public.

10 November – 13 January
'**Becks Futures 2**' exhibition of the annual art prize for emerging artists at the Laing Art Gallery, Newcastle.
(Participating artists: Shahin Afrassiabi, Fabienne Audéoud & John Russell, Simon Bill, David Burrows, Brian Griffiths, Dan Holdsworth, Gemma Iles, DJ Simpson, Tim Stoner and Clare Woods.)

The Arc in Stockton closes after being forced into liquidation caused by failure to meet income targets for ticket sales. Northern Arts enter into discussions with Stockton Borough Council and arts organisations in the Tees Valley to discuss how the building might be saved.

13 November (– 5 December)
The exhibition '**The Developing Process: The Pasmore Pavilion**' opens at the Architectural Association in London. The exhibition takes place against a backdrop of debates about the future of Pasmore's *Apollo Pavilion*, now under threat of demolition and the victim of graffiti and other vandalism, due to a lack of maintenance over the years.

22 November
Opening of the new £31m **British Galleries** at the Victoria and Albert Museum, London (and the abolition of entrance fees to the museum).

Drawing of *Producers* speakers, 14 November 2001, by Suzy Wandless.

2 – 7 October
Berlin Art Forum, BALTIC press launch.

14 November
The Producers:
Mark Nash and **Ute Meta Bauer** in conversation, University of Newcastle.

5 December
The Producers:
Jeremy Millar and **Teresa Gleadowe** in conversation, University of Newcastle.

12 January – 2 March
Francis Gomila's video installation *A Place called Oxmoor* is shown at Artists' Space in New York.

25 January
The **Blue Carpet**, a new public square designed by the Thomas Heatherwick Studio, is unveiled outside the Laing Art Gallery in Newcastle City Centre.

Comprising a 'carpet' of purpose-made blue glass tiles and incorporating seating, the square is described as a 'visually thrilling but completely functional urban space' and is the source of much discussion about the intensity of its blue colour at its unveiling in January.

18 February
The **National Portrait Gallery**, London, announces its plan to open a regional outpost in Durham.

9 February – 7 March
'Life is Beautiful'
An exhibition curated by Andrew Patrizio at the Laing Art Gallery, Newcastle.

Includes work by artists Richard Deacon, Felix Gonzales-Torres, Ian Hamilton Finlay and Marc Quinn.

March
Anish Kapoor (commissioned by BALTIC in 1999) is announced as the third artist to be commissioned to make a work for Tate Modern's Turbine Hall, as part of the Unilever Series of commissions. Previous commissions in the Series awarded to Louise Bourgeois, 2000, and Juan Muñoz, 2001.

7 March – 6 April
Natalie Frost, *Man-Trap*: an installation by former BALTIC Artist-in-Residence at Waygood Gallery, Newcastle.

2002

7 January
Removal of scaffolding on east façade of BALTIC building begins.

16 January
The Producers:
Sacha Craddock and **Andrew Renton** in conversation.

5 February
The Producers:
Laura Godfrey-Isaacs and **Jonathan Watkins** in conversation.

6 March
The Producers:
Barbara London and **James Putnam** in conversation.

March
Removal of final interior and exterior scaffolding from BALTIC building.

5–9 March
Stockholm Art Fair, BALTIC press launch.

9 March
Building delays cause BALTIC's planned opening on 9 March to be postponed.

Joseph No.8 awarded to Åke Axelsson, designer of the BALTIC furniture.

Pupils from John Spence Community High School, North Shields, take part in a football/dance/poetry workshop at the Newcastle United football ground for two participatory projects devised by BALTIC visiting artist **Alec Finlay** (*Football Haiku* and *Labanotation: That Gemmill Goal!*). See *Football Haiku* and *Labanotation: the Archie Gemmill Goal*, two books by artist and publisher-in-residence Alec Finlay; co-published by BALTIC, pocketbooks and Morning Star. *Labanotation* includes dance performances by local school children, photographed at St. James, Park.)

Also published this spring: *Irish 2*, by Alec Finlay, Guy Moreton and Zoe Irvine, with photographs of the path to the Wittgenstein house on Skjolden, Norway. Co-published by BALTIC, Morning Star and SPACEX.

Labanotation and *Football Haiku* workshops led by Andy Howitt and Ken Cockburn, March 2002. Photos: Guy Moreton.

Natalie Frost,
Man-Trap (detail)
2002.

7 March
Northern Arts announce
£180,000 of investment for the
re-opening of Arc in Stockton.

16 March – 13 April
CAPITAL
A month-long series of exhibitions
and site-specific works across
Newcastle, involving twenty-seven
artists based in the North East.
Each artist is invited to examine
the relationship to identity, history
and different cultures of the city.
'CAPITAL' is also the first project
from VANE as a formally consti-
tuted visual arts organisation.

Natalie Frost, *More!*, neon
sign on the wall of Holy
Jesus Hospital, Newcastle,
as part of 'CAPITAL'.

19 March
Erection of the wing door on
glazed east façade of the building.
This sliding, teflon-coated door is
almost the full height of the building. It will be used to control light
levels in the art spaces, acting as
a screen when closed.

TV Swansong launch at Sunderland
Road Library, Gateshead.

20 March
TV Swansong: eight commissions with live webcast, curated
by Karen Guthrie & Nina Pope,
including public internet access
at BALTIC Learning Centre,
Sunderland Road Library,
Gateshead.

Wing Door being lifted into place
at BALTIC, March 2002.
Image courtesy Gateshead Council.

Through **[a-n] MAGAZINE**, www.anweb.co.uk and a lively programme of artists' events, [a-n] THE ARTISTS' INFORMATION COMPANY, based in Newcastle, presents a UK and international perspective on artists and changing visual arts practices.

Northern Print Studio, in collaboration with PEALS and the Hatton Gallery, win the Wellcome Trust Sci-art award. Commissioned artists: Shona Illingworth, Ashley McCormick, Daniel Sturgis and Louise K. Wilson.

26–27 March
Newcastle and Gateshead launch their joint bid for the 2008 **European City of Culture** with two evenings of projections on BALTIC.

1 April
Northern Arts, one of the prime advocates for a new international exhibition gallery in Tyneside, along with the other English Regional Arts Boards, join the Arts Council of England to form a single development organisation for the arts in England.

The **Metro** extension to Sunderland creates a new phase

in the Nexus **Art in Transport programme**, with works such as Simon Watkinson's *Electrolyte II* (Park Lane Bus Interchange, Sunderland, 2000) and Morag Morrison's *Sunderland Direct Colour Strategy* (2000–2001).

May
Waygood Gallery and Studios (currently housing 25 artists' studios) negotiates a twenty-five year lease with Newcastle City Council, who also purchase Waygood's five-floor warehouse. This partnership will result in a new artist-centred cultural venue, devised and managed by Waygood, due to open in 2005. The venue will provide studios and workshops

for forty artists, a new ground floor gallery and accommodation for other cultural organisations.

25 May
Manchester City Art Gallery re-opens after a four-year closure and a £35 million expansion and refurbishment. The scheme, which doubles the gallery's display space, links the original 1834 building with the former Athenaeum and a new wing designed by Sir Michael Hopkins.
The inaugural exhibition is 'Inhale/Exhale': an installation by Michael Craig Martin.

BALTIC opening date & programme projections, 3 April 2002.

3 April
BALTIC announces its **opening date (Saturday 13 July)** and

B.OPEN programme with a series of projections onto the north façade of the building.

April
Publication of B.READ/SIX: *Curating New Media*.

Spring
Installation of arts lift.
The lift (105m³ with a load bearing capacity of 10 tonnes) is the largest of its kind in the UK, and allows for artworks to be transported to any art space in the building.

Installation of three panoramic lifts on the west façade of the building.

7 May
As part of the celebrations surrounding her Golden Jubilee, **The Queen** visits the North East, where she officially opens the Sunderland Metro link and the Gateshead Millennium Bridge. She also visits BALTIC prior to its opening in July.

15 June
Kurt Schwitters and the MerzBarn in Cumbria
A public seminar at Elterwater, Cumbria, organised by the Kurt Schwitters working group (set up to research and promote the work of Kurt Schwitters in England). Speakers include Fred Brookes and Mary Burkett, former Director of Abbot Hall Art Gallery, Kendal.

June–September
Documenta11, Kassel, Germany.
Artistic Director: Okwui Enwezor.
Co-curators: Carlos Basualdo, Ute Meta Bauer, Susanne Ghez, Sarat Maharaj, Mark Nash and Octavio Zaya.

15 May – 14 July
(The World May Be)
Fantastic, Sydney Biennale, Australia.
Artistic Director: Richard Grayson (former member of Newcastle's Basement Group).

The Queen signs the guest book at BALTIC, 7 May 2002.

14 May
Artist **Tatsumi Orimoto** talks about his *Breadman* performances at the Universities of Newcastle and Northumbria, and Newcastle College.

29 June
Family and friends **test the building day**.
Over 1000 people are invited to BALTIC in advance of the official public opening on 13 July.

BALTIC Newsletter No.16, with cover designed by Julian Opie.

BALTIC Newsletter No.16
published
The final BALTIC Newsletter, No.16, is an exhibition guide to 'B.OPEN'.

13 July
BALTIC opens to the public.
The opening displays, 'B.OPEN',
are intended to show the full
potential of the building and to
make manifest the concept of an
Art Factory. The artists involved
in the B.OPEN programme are
Chris Burden, Carsten Höller,
Julian Opie, Jaume Plensa,
Jane & Louise Wilson, Tatsumi
Orimoto, Anna Bjerge Hansen and
in the studios, Los Carpinteros,
Alec Finlay, Eva Grubinger, Chad
McCail and Tsuyoshi Osawa.

BALTIC staff, spring 2002.
From left to right: Sune Nordgren,
Wendy Lothian, Chris Osborne, Keith Jupp,
Tom Cullen, Anne Howes, Sarah Martin,
Alec Finlay, Fiona O'Connor, Sarah
Hudspeth, Jude Watt, Hannah Civico,
Angela Hedley, John Smith, Alsion Scott,
Emma Thomas, Andy Walker, Stephen
Cleland, Sophie Thomson, Jo Wilson,
Vicki Lewis. (not pictured: Viv Anderson,
Stuart Harris, James Johnson, Sara Ley,
Elliott Young.)
Photo: Etienne Clément, 2002
© Etienne Clément

BALTIC Building Facts and Figures

Funding:
Total Project Cost: £45.7 million
Construction Cost: £24.8 million
(£33.4 million from the National
Lottery through the Arts Council of
England;
BALTIC is the first Lottery funded
project to be awarded revenue funding
of £1.5m a year for five years.)

Funders:
The National Lottery through the
Arts Council of England
Gateshead Council
Northern Arts
English Partnerships through One
North East
European Regional Development
Fund

Design Concept (A summary):
The Baltic Flour Mills was a disused silo building sited on the south bank of the River Tyne in Gateshead. The architectural proposal can be summarised as the hollowing out of the existing internal silo structure and the opening of the east and west walls, leaving parallel monolithic brick walls to the north and south.

BALTIC is comprised of two components, the two-storey Riverside Building (the main entrance to BALTIC) and the Main Building. The Main Building is the redeveloped 1950s industrial brick building of which the north and south facades have been maintained. A new structure consisting of six main floors and three mezzanines has been secured between these facades and containing BALTIC's five Art Spaces. Glass is used to create the east and west elevations providing a natural light source and capitalising on the exceptional views the site offers to Tyneside and the surrounding area.

One of the principal themes running through the design evolution was to retain the verticality of the existing building and to emphasise its impressive presence on the Quayside. The views out from the building to the surrounding cityscape were important, as were the creation of simple, large-scale spaces that could be easily reconfigured for exhibitions and other events. The vertical nature of the building and the arrangement of the gallery floors in this way gives the building a high level of flexibility in the opening and closing of gallery spaces: important for the highly unpredictable nature of contemporary art. **Dominic Williams, Architect.**

The Building:
- The existing building structure is 25m wide, 52m long and 42m high.
- The building originally contained 148, 2.5m^2 concrete grain silos, held in place between solid brick walls. The silos were surgically removed in 1998–99

(the 'enabling works'). During the enabling works, the brick façades to the north and south were supported within a steel scaffolding cage, which was in turn supported off the existing slab foundation.
- The 4 towers (one at each corner of the building) were originally empty. In the new building, the towers or 'cores' are used to house public and back of house staircases and the arts lift, and have been completed in Cor-Ten steel.

The New Building:
- Net internal floor area (Gallery Building): 8537m^2.
- Net internal floor area (Riverside Building): 1442m^2.
- Total arts programme space: 3290m^2.
- The 4 main concrete floors (based on the original silo grid) are designed to take 6 tonne point loadings.
- The main gallery building can accommodate up to 1700 people at any one time.

Ground Floor
- Ground Floor Art Space: 244m^2 and 4.5m high.
  The only art space in the building with a slate (rather than a wooden) floor. Connected to artists' workshops, also at ground level.

Level 1
- Total floor area of Level 1: 510m^2
- Level 1 Art Space: 324m^2 and 7.4m high, with additional backstage area of 68m^2 and 5.5m high.
  Level 1 Art Space is a flexible art, project and event space. Functions include live art space, screening room,

gallery, auditorium and conference space. The space has capacity for up to 300 people (seated), is semi acoustically isolated and has a full theatrical lighting rig.
- Cinema/auditorium: 53m². Fully acoustically isolated with seating for 54 people.
- Cube: A 53m² 'black box', with facility for projection onto the 4 walls, the ceiling and the floor.

Level 1A
- Media Lab: 110m² and 2.15m high.

Media Lab Resources:
Video:
3 x Mediq 100 loss less quality Video edit systems
1 x Ice effects machine (for after effects)
2 x Portable video edit systems base on final cut pro and cinewave card
Digibeta and DVCpro broadcast cameras
Video transfer facilities: transfer from different formats and countries to UK standards

Audio:
1 x Protools digital audio edit system
1 x Digital multi-track system

3D Design: various 3D software packages including softimage and Maya

Graphics: Graphics packages include PhotoShop, illustrator and Flash

Level 2
- Level 2 Art Space: 182m² and 5.5m high.
- Library: 93m² and 2.3m high.
- Archive: 52m² and 2.3m high.

Level 2A
- Office/Administration Space: 413m²

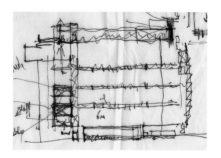

Level 3
- Level 3 Art Space: 745m² and 4.4m high.
  With full environmental control, designed to meet Museum and Gallery Commission specifications.

Level 4
- Level 4 Art Space: 745m² and 8.5m high.
  With natural light through roof glazing panels.

Level 5/6
- Viewing Box: 135m²
  The Viewing Box is a glazed, double-height space clad in anodised aluminium that cantilevers out 7m from the west façade of the Main Building. Can accommodate up to 70 people on two-levels.

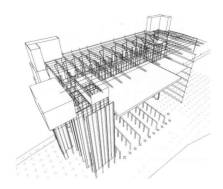

Level 6:
- Rooftop Restaurant: 280m²
  A 'glass box' suspended between the four towers of the building.
  The restaurant level is formed from trussed steelwork, with diagonally-braced external bays and a movement-resisting frame in the central bay.

Artists' Studios:
- The 3 studio spaces are located in the receiving house (on the north-west corner of the building):
  AIR 1: Ground Floor; 64m² and 4m high.
  AIR 2: Level 1A; 55m².
  AIR 3: Level 2; 55m².

Education Spaces:
- Ground Floor Mezzanine Studio
- Level 1 Studio
  (Both spaces 45m² and 2.5m high)

Riverside Building:
- Bookshop: 170m²
- Riverside Café/Bar: 130m²
- Riverside Restaurant: 255m²
  The roof of the Riverside Building cantilevers out 7m into Baltic Square, to provide an entrance canopy.

Materials and Finishes:
- Lightweight anodised aluminium panels: used externally to clad new parts of the building, including the Viewing Box and the roof of the Riverside Building.
- Cor-Ten steel panels: used to reform existing or missing parts of the original brick structure, including the towers at each corner. Cor-Ten is also used for the interior of the Riverside Building.
- Slate: Ffestiniog slate used for the Ground Floor Art Space and the back wall of the Riverside Café/Bar.
- Swedish pine: used for floor surfaces in all Art Spaces (apart from Ground Floor),

artists' studios, the Rooftop Restaurant and the administration level.)

- Glass: Used for the east and west façades of the building; the roof of the Level 4 Art Space; the west wall of the Viewing Box; the walls of the Rooftop Restaurant and the east wall of the Ladies' toilets on Level 6.

Structure:

- The devised structural solution allows for flexibility, whilst maintaining the integrity of the structure.
- Reduced fin walls provide stability to the perimeter walls under wind loading. The main vertical load-bearing elements are 'T' shaped reinforced concrete columns based on the original 2.5m² silo grid.
- Stability is also provided by the existing towers at the 4 corners of the building.
- The Rooftop Restaurant floor is supported by a series of stainless steel cast fork frames which span between the north and south walls. This light-weight structure was designed to allow daylight to pass through the lay lights to the high gallery space.

Environmental Engineering:

- All designs for the building systems have been strongly influenced by environmental considerations.
- A stand-alone Energy Centre to the east contains all the primary plant, including a Combined Heat and Power unit, which saves dramatically on energy consumption.
- The building's thermal mass is used to limit summertime temperatures and daylight is carefully controlled.
- A void at the front of the west end provides a natural stack air movement throughout the public spaces.
- Displacement ventilation is used in majority of Art Spaces, providing low

velocity heated or cooled air at low level, through grills in the floors.
- A computerised management system is used to control levels of heat, security, lighting, air conditioning and energy use in the building.

Lighting:

- Daylight is brought into the building through the east and west façades (with a blind system for control of natural light), and through roof glazing on Level 4. The wing door can also be closed off to prevent daylight entering through the east façade.
- A suspended fabric ceiling (on Levels 2 & 3), with lighting battens above, provides ambient background lighting. Between the panels of the fabric ceiling, a flexible spot track grid is suspended for accent lighting.
- The ambient light crosses in the ground Floor and Level 4 Art Spaces ghost the original silo grid whilst creating even light spread.

- All the lighting can be controlled in the art spaces using hand-held computers for scene setting and dimming.
- BALTIC has entered into a partnership with lighting consultant John Johnson and lighting company DAL (Designed Architectural Lighting) to design a multi-purpose and user-friendly gallery lighting unit especially for the BALTIC art spaces.

Design Features:

- 3 glazed, 21-person lifts on the west façade, travel to each floor of the building at a speed of 2 meters-per-second.
- Wing Door: 21m high. Weight: 11 tonnes. A teflon-coated door on the east façade that slides across to screen out daylight, when required.
- Arts Lift: 21m² and 5m high. Capacity: 10 tonnes. Can transport work to any of the 4 main gallery floors.
- The main public staircase (housed in the tower on BALTIC's south-west corner) has internal glazing, providing views into each floor, and has a central void running the whole height of the building.
- The original receiving house attached to the main building now houses a series of education and artist spaces that benefit from natural daylight and ventilation. The roof provides an external public terrace that can be accessed from the Level 4 Art Space.
- The building houses 18 purpose-designed, fully accessible WC facilities.
- There are 2 further 13-person lifts for use by staff and artists.

Gateshead Metropolitan Borough Council – BALTIC Flour Mills Arts Brief – April 1994

Our objective in the development and conversion of Baltic Flour Mills is to provide a national and international centre for contemporary visual arts with large temporary exhibition spaces. Both in scale and artistic policy it would be unique in this country and one of only half a dozen comparable facilities in the world.

Relevant international comparators, which should inform architectural proposals for Baltic Flour Mills are the Museums of Contemporary Art in Chicago, Tokyo and Los Angeles (perhaps especially the Temporary Contemporary galleries in the latter), through to the Hallen für Neue Kunst, Shaffhausen Collection, in Switzerland, or the Mattress Factory in Pittsburgh. Also of interest are the flour mill recently converted to a contemporary gallery in Oporto, and the Bankside Power Station Southwark, London, being considered for the Tate's Museum of Modern Art.

Contemporary visual artists require large spaces for their works to be seen at their best and this fact is reflected internationally in buildings and building conversions which provide exhibitions and related exhibition work to develop and extend the appreciation of the work of living artists. Large-scale temporary installations are common in this field of practice, as are media-based installations by artists working in video and interactive systems.

The Building
The Baltic Flour Mills is situated on the south side of the River Tyne. It has a dominant position within the landscape

(especially viewed from the redeveloped Newcastle Quayside) because of its size and position. From it, there are wonderful views of the Tyne bridges – especially from roof level.

The building contains approximately 1.5 million cubic feet of space and extends to a height of over 130 feet. An initial study of the building has suggested it may contain just four gallery floors (approx. 100 ft x 80 ft with heights of 15 ft, 20 ft, 20 ft and 30ft) with an entrance floor containing meeting rooms, studios, library, retail, display and reception areas. Other solutions are of course possible (including office space) but the building must be primarily dedicated to exhibition space and related facilities. Roof level cafeteria and viewing areas, exterior ground floor concourse and the usual service area; e.g. adequate loading bays and lifts, and car parking, are desired requirements.

Environmental controls would vary according to the exhibits, so a flexible and cost-effective system of environmental control is needed. Similarly, lighting systems should be flexible.

To preserve the character and integrity of the building, it is felt that the north and south facades should be largely retained. A programme of commissioned artworks for the exterior concourse is likely to be implemented both during the development of the building and thereafter.

Visual Arts Year 1996
We attach great importance to our aspiration to have at least part of the building temporarily open to the public in early 1996, when the northern region celebrates UK Visual Arts Year. We are currently negotiating the British Art Show tour at that time. We are therefore keen to know if a 'fast track' solution in the development is possible that would enable at least one floor with a minimum height of 30ft to be able to accommodate a public exhibition for part of 1996 – no special environmental controls would be required. Tenders should therefore be based on a phasing programme to allow for this. The Developer will therefore realise that the solution addresses this point and also the estimate final cost of the project, bearing in mind these restrictions.

The matter of structural stability both during construction and on completion must be carefully illustrated in any submission.

BALTIC Design Team

Client:
Gateshead Council

Architects:
Ellis Williams Architects, London

Contractor (Enabling Works):
Nuttalls Construction Ltd.
Contractor (Construction Works):
HBG Construction North East Ltd.

Gateshead Council, Department of Architectural Services:
John Devlin (Director)
Peter Udall (Major Projects Manager)
John Anderson (Project Manager)
David Hosken (Finance Monitoring Officer)
Michelle Pilkington (Senior Support Assistant)
Bernie Forster (Construction Project Manager)

Ellis Williams Architects:
EWA Directors wish to thank the following individuals from the design team who made a real commitment to the project during the eight years it took from its inception in April 1994 to the present: Kate Sandle, who assisted on original stage two competition drawings with the addition of Martin Edwards, Jason Geen and Sarah Williams for the Lottery bid stage in 1996 which saw the inclusion of the Riverside Building. The team increased significantly in size for the production drawings, the members of which are included in the list below. The final long and difficult site stage required very special people to see it through from September 1998. These included, amongst others, Keith Jupp and a truly determined duo, Jason Geen and Iain Fairbairn. The quality of the building is a testament to these key individuals.

Ellis Williams Architects:
John Adden (Director)
Tim Baker (Director)
Nicola Brennan
Pat Bonfield
Michael Cheung
Steve Citrone
Rosemary Curry

Martin Edwards
Iain Fairbairn
Rob Freeman
Jason Geen
Simon Groves

Keith Jupp
Niall Maxwell
Henry Ng
Katrina Plews
Katrin Sachs
Kate Sandle
Fritz Stoll
Dominic Williams (Director)
Matt Williams
Mariq Wojciechowski
James Wright

Thanks also to the following individuals from engineering, arts, construction and graphics disciplines who contributed in many different ways to the design development: Scobie Alvis; Alan Arnott; Bridge Ltd.; John Corps; Assim Khan (Stage 1 competition concept engineer); Pat Mcdonald; Richard Nightingale; Julian Opie; Richard La Trobe Bateman; Charles Walker and Richard Wilson.

Consultant Company lists
Boyden and Company: Cost consultants
John Forester
Gavin Charlesworth
Kevin Daglish
Colin Hayward
Bruce McPate

Atelier One: Structural Engineers
Chris Brown
Scott Nelson
Tanya Scotnie
Derek Speirs
Neil Thomas

Atelier Ten: Environmental engineers
Mike Reece
RudiDuncan-Bosu,
Mark Delamaine
Steve Marshall
Patrick Bellew

Arup Lighting: Lighting Consultants
Florence Lam
Arfon Davies

AAD: Acoustic consultants
Mark Bishop

Warrington fire research: Fire engineers
Terry Ashton

Burdus Access Management: Access consultants
David Burdus
Steve Hudson

References – Art/Architectural Works

The Cummins Factory, Darlington
The US-based Cummins Engine Company built its own UK factory in Darlington in 1965. Designed by American architects Kevin Roche and John Dinkeloo and Associates, the 10,000 sq ft building was widely acclaimed at the time and was later given Grade II listed status. In the mid-1990s Cummins relocated to Darlington and the factory put up for sale. By June 2000 Orange had bought the building and refitted it to be the 'most technically advanced communications centre in Europe'.

Antony Gormley, *Angel of the North*, Gateshead, 1998
Commissioned by Gateshead Council, the 200 tonne sculpture is 20 metres high and has a wingspan of 54 metres. Fabricated in Hartlepool and made of weather resistant Cor-Ten steel, the *Angel* stands on a hillside near the A1 in Gateshead where it is seen by an estimated 90,000 people each day.

Gunnar Asplund, The Stockholm City Library
The Stockholm City Library was completed between 1924 and 1927. The form of this building, with its circular reading room surrounded by a cubic structure, is informed both by studies of contemporary American public libraries and by Danish neo-classicism. The library is one of the first pieces of architecture to give the classical forms and rational thinking of the Enlightenment project a more modest and human scale.

Chris Burden
See for example, Chris Burden, *Chris Burden: A Twenty-Year Survey*, (Orange County Museum of Art, 1988).

Baltic Memories
Baltic Memories was an exhibition celebrating the work of people at the Baltic Flour Mills. It was organised by BALTIC in collaboration with Gateshead Council Arts and Libraries Department and Tyne and Wear Museums, at the Shipley Art Gallery, Gateshead (May-June 1999). An accompanying documentary film was made by A19 Film and Video.

c/Plex Centre, West Bromwich, Sandwell
The Jubilee Arts c/PLEX project is a new centre for artistic innovation in community arts practice; bridging the arts, community and technology, due to open in 2004 in a new building designed by Alsop Architects.

Janet Cardiff, *Forty Part Motet*, (2001), Castle Keep, Newcastle
Commissioned by Field with the Arts Council of England; Canada House; The Salisbury Festival and the Salisbury Cathedral Choir; BALTIC, The New Art Gallery, Walsall; the NOW Festival Nottingham.

Etienne Clément
See for example, *BALTIC: A Vision on Emulsion: Photographs by Etienne Clément*, RIBA, London, (February–March 2002).

Neil Cummings and Marysia Lewandowska, *Capital*, the inaugural project in the Contemporary Interventions series at Tate Modern, (May–September 2001).

Gateshead Car Park, Gateshead, was designed by Owen Luder in the late-1960's.

The **Ikon Gallery, Birmingham**, (1999), designed by architects Levitt Bernstein in collaboration with artist Tania Kovats.

Anish Kapoor, *TARATANTARA*, BALTIC, (July–September 1999).

The **New Art Gallery, Walsall**, (2000), designed by architects, Caruso St John.

Julian Opie, see for example, Lynne Cooke (ed.), *Julian Opie*, (London: Thames & Hudson, 1994) and *Julian Opie*, (Ikon Gallery, Birmingham, 2001).

Jaume Plensa, *Blake in Gateshead*, as part of the 'Temporary Contemporary', BALTIC, (1996).

PS1 (Public School 1) is an art space housed in an old school building, situated in Queen's, New York.

'**No Socks: Kurt Schwitters and the *MerzBarn***', Hatton Gallery, Newcastle (April–May 1999).

Tate Modern, London, (2000) is housed in the former Bankside Power Station, London, designed by Giles Gilbert Scott and converted by architects Herzog and de Meuron.

Martín Weber, photographs from the 'Dream Series', Side Gallery, Newcastle, (2001).

Malmö Konsthall, Malmö, (1975). Re-opened, with a renovation designed by architect Klas Anselm, in April 1994.

The Wapping Project, London, (2000) is a new space for art in a disused, steam-powered hydraulic pumping station on the Wapping Wall, designed by architects Shed 54 and artistic director, Jules Wright.

Films
Mike Hodges, *Get Carter*, (1971).
Spike Jonze, *Being John Malkovich*, (1999).
Terry Gilliam, *Brazil*, (1985).

Written Works/Books
As It Is, (Birmingham: Ikon Gallery, 2000).

The **BALTIC Newsletter**, Issue 1 published November 1998. The BALTIC Newsletter has been published approximately every 2/3 months, culminatin gin the final issue, No.16, published in July 2002 to celebrate the opening of BALTIC.

Michel de Certeau, *Walking in the City, The Practice of Everyday Life*, (Berkeley: University of California Press, 1984), pp.92–110.

Alex Coles (ed.), *Site Specificity: the Ethnographic Turn*, (London: Black Dog Publishing, 2001).

Peter Collymore, *The Architecture of Ralph Erskine*, (London: Architext, 1982).

Douglas Crimp, 'On The Museum's Ruins', Hal Foster (ed.), *Postmodern Culture*, (UK, Pluto Press, 1985), pp.43–56.

Neil Cummings and Marysia Lewandowska, *The Value of Things*, (London: August Publications, 2001).

'**Give and Take**', (London, Victoria and Albert Museum and the Serpentine Gallery, London, 2001).

Jonathan Hill (ed.), *Occupying Architecture*, (London: Routledge, 1998).

De Oliviera, Oxley, Petry (eds.), *Installation Art*, (London: Thames and Hudson, 1994).

Nick Kaye, *Site-Specific Art: Performance, Place And Documentation*, (London: Routledge, 2000)

Sarah Martin and Sune Nordgren (eds.), *New Sites – New Art*, B.Read/One, (Gateshead: BALTIC, 2000).

Susan Hiller and Sarah Martin (eds.) *The Producers: Contemporary Curators in Conversation*, B.Read /Two, (BALTIC, 2000).

Sarah Martin and Sune Nordgren (eds.), *Artists at Work*, B.Read /Three, (BALTIC, 2001).

Susan Hiller and Sarah Martin (eds.), The Producers: Contemporary Curators in Conversation (2), B.Read /Four, (BALTIC, 2001).

Victoria Newhouse, *Towards a New Museum*, (New York: The Monacelli Press, 1998).

Nicolas de Oliveira, Nicola Oxley, Michael Petry, with texts by Michael Archer, *Out Of Here: Creative Collaborations Beyond The Gallery*, (Birmingham: Ikon Gallery, 1997).

Georg Simmel, 'Bridge and Door', in Neil Leach (ed.), *Rethinking Architecture*, (London: Routledge, 1997), pp.66–8.

Jane Rendell, 'Conductor: a tribute to the angels', catalogue essay for artist Jane Prophet's *Conductor* at Wapping, London, 2000, (December 2000).

Jane Rendell, 'Longing for the Lightness of Spring', catalogue essay for artist Elina Brotherus' installation at Wapping, London, 2001, (October 2001).

Jane Rendell, 'Imagination is the Root of all Change', *Bridges*, (a book accompanying three films on bridges by Lucy Blakstad), (London: August Publications, 2001).

Gavin Wade (ed.), *Curating in the 21st Century*, (New Art Gallery Walsall/ University of Wolverhampton, 2000).

Web-Sites
www.abbeymedia.com/Janweb/
www.balticmill.com/
www.c-plex.co.uk/
www.archinet.co.uk/elliswilliams/
www.gateshead.gov.uk/
dspace.dial.pipex.com/ikon/
www.konsthall.malmo.se/
www.north.org.uk/
www.ps1.org/
www.tate.org.uk/

Baltic Flour Mills Visual Arts Trust

BALTIC Staff and Crew

Staff

Sune Nordgren
Director

Vicki Lewis
Deputy Director/Curator

Viv Anderson
Workshop Technician

Hannah Civico
Marketing Officer

Stephen Cleland
Finance Manager

Tom Cullen
Multi-Media Manager

Stuart Harris
Audio Visual Officer

Angela Hedley
Finance Officer

Anne Howes
Assistant to the Director

Sarah Hudspeth
Press Officer

James Johnson
Building Services

Keith Jupp
Building Co-ordinator

Sara Ley
Bookshop/Retail Officer

Wendy Lothian
Programme Co-ordinator

Sarah Martin
Assistant Curator

Fiona O'Connor
Fundraiser

Chris Osborne
Technical Manager

Alison Scott
Strategic Planning

John Smith
Gallery Technician

Emma Thomas
Education and Public Programme
Manager

Sophie Thomson
Education and Public Programme

Andy Walker
Strategic Planning

Jude Watt
Education and Public Programme

Jo Wilson
Marketing and Development
Manager

Elliott Young
IT Officer

BALTIC Crew

Paula Adams
Gemma Bailey
Neela Basu
Eva Bauer
Megan Beddell
James Boaden
Sarah Bouttell
Deena Bowman
Nick Clark
Alison Cleland
John Cuthbert
Karen Davies
Darren Garrett
Victoria Gill
Ian Gonczarow
Amanda Gould
Laura Harrington
Brooke Hedley
Laura Hewitt
Andrew Hodson
Pauline Holland
Beatrice Hussain
Ben Jones
Manika Karlsson
Amanda Kennington
Mari Kilner
Kath Kingsbury
Roisin Lightfoot
Philippa Little
Andrea Macdonald
Victoria Marcontonio
Mireille Martel
Melissa Murphy
Sarah Noble
Mark O'Kane
Lesley Richardson
Alex Ryley

Melanie Schofield
Andy Sheridan
Beth Sibbald
Rebecca Simmonds
Jenny Snell
Lee Stokoe
Sheila Thompson
Miles Thurlow
Ian Tinwell
Sarah Turnbull
Lianne Vollans
Christo Wallers
Anita Wan
Ian Watson
Iain Wheeldon
Rosie Wilson
Joy Woolley

Acknowledgments

BALTIC would like to thank the following individuals and organisations whose hard work, advice, collaboration and support has been invaluable to the development of the project:

A19 Film and Video (Belinda Williams and Nick Oldham); AIRS; Dave Abbott; Charlotte Åberg; Absolute Leisure; Julie Allison; Marjorie Allthorpe-Guyton; Mike Andrews; Lynette Ardis; Tuula Arkio; Emma Armstrong; Åke Axelsson; Mike Aynsley; Bill Baird; Christopher Bailey; Helen Baker-Alder; Tamas Banovich; Karolynne Barker; Jerry Barford; Christian Barnes; Dan Beard; Linda Bell; Tory Bender; Marcus Bennett; Theresa Bergne; Catherine Bertola; Peter Berwick; Anna Best; Jon Bewley and Simon Herbet (Locus+); Maura Biava; Daniel Birnbaum; Ian Blackwell; Blakes Coffee Shop; Ingrid Blanco Diaz; Neville Blaszk; Richard Bliss; Cherri Blisset; Marente Bloemheuvel; Pat Blue; Bolden Farmhouse Pantry; Peter Bolger; Stefania Bonelli; Jacqui Boyd; Fred Brookes; Nick Broomhall (Audi UK); Dave Bunce; Chris Burden; Mary E Burkett; Ronnie Burn; Andrew Burton; James Bustard; David Butler; Guy Brett; Jennie Callaghan; Mike Campbell; Shirley Campbell; Eileen Carnaffin; Los Carpinteros (Alexandre Arrechea, Marco Castillo, Dagoberto Rodriguez); Alison Carter; Sandy Carter; Carolyn Christov-Bakargiev; Rupert Clamp; Judith Clancey; Ian Clarkin; Classic Masonry; Etienne Clément; Clyde Canvas;

Janet Cardiff; John Clayson; Derek Coates; Mike Collier; Stephen Collins; Jed Connaly; Sarah Cook; Carol Cooke; Lynne Cooke; Moss Cooper; Richard Cork; Lisa Corrin; Vuk Cosic; Jo Coupe; Brian Cox; Cox and Wyman (Ruth Goodman and Jo House); Sacha Craddock; Anne Curtis; Lynn Cuthbert; Mark Daniels; Peter Davies; Suzanne Davies; Brian Davison; Richard Deacon; Dean Taxis; Jan Debbaut; Ravi Deepres; Nick Devlin; Disability Gateshead; Andrew Dixon; Claire Dixon; Mark Dobson; Nick Dolan; Chris Dorsett; Jennifer Douglas; Judith Douthwaite; Tony Durcan; Carolyn Earlam; David Elliott; Fiona Ellis (Northern Rock Foundation); Thomas Elovsson; Les Elton; Charles Esche; Andreas Fahlstedt; David Faulkner; Alec Finlay; Mary Flemming; Diane Fisher-Naylor; John Flynn; Martin Forster; Friselle, Venice; Natalie Frost; Chris Galloway; Matthew Gansallo; Gateshead College; Alanna Gedgaudas; Kees van Gelder; Peter Geschwind; Councillor George Gill; George Gillespie; Liam Gillick; Teresa Gleadowe; Peter Glazinski; Felix Gmelin; David Goard; Laura Godfrey-Isaacs; Francis Gomila; Maggie Goodbarn; Beryl Graham; Bob Graham; Gloria Graham; Polly Gray; Richard Grayson; Simon Grennan & Christopher Sperandio; Kris Grey; Eva Grubinger; Jaap Guldemond; Timandra Gustafson; Karen Guthrie & Nina Pope; Antoinette Hächler; Ken Haigh; Canon Bill Hall; Nigel Hall; Anne Bjerge Hansen; Tod Hanson;

Tony Harrington; Hatton Gallery, Newcastle; Hargreaves Foundry, Halifax; Harkness Hall Ltd.; Maureen Harries; Hays Travel, Gateshead; Matthew Hearn; Hedleys Humpers; Peter Hewitt; Matthew Higgs; Susan Hiller; Ruth Hill; Tony Hindhaugh; Jennifer Hinves; Michelle Hirschhorn; Hobsbawm Macauley Communications Ltd. (Helen Scott Lidget, Jessica Ray, Ben Rawlinson Plant); Carsten Höller; Jenny Holzer; Angela Horn; David Hosken; Angela Hudson; Ian Hunter; Fiona Holmes; Kevin Hunter; ISIS Arts; Karen James; Keith Jeffrey; Peter Jenkinson; Ken Jobling; Thora Johansen; yr 7, 8 and 9 pupils at John Spence Community High School; Catherine Johns; John Johnson; Stuart Johnson; Eric Jubb; Brigitte Jurack; Kathryn Kanjo; Anish Kapoor; Thomas Karlsson; Sharon Kivland; Roger Kelly; Vanessa Kelly; Maureen Kestevan; Mike Kirkup; Wendy Kirkup; Gunilla Klingberg; Franz König; Pascale Konyn; Jaap Kroneman; Martin Ladds; Barry Lamb; Catherine Lampert; Caroline Larkin; Heather Lee; Herman Lelie; George Lewis; Therese Lewis; James Lingwood; Zoe Linsley; Lisson Gallery, London; Mark Little; The Little Theatre, Gateshead; Andrea Lloyd; John Lloyd; Doreen Livingstone; Nicholas Logsdail; Alf Longhurst; Barbara London; Sue Lovell; Joan Lowery; Owen Luder; Joanne Luther; Joyce MacKenzie; Bill MacNaught; Keith McIntyre; Russell Mclean; Joanne McLeod; Andrew Maidwell (Colebrook Audi); Makers and Shakers; Makro, Washington; Lena Malm; Malmaison Hotel, Newcastle; Atillio Maranzano; Rhiannon Mason; Toby Mason; Malcolm Mather; Ebba Matz; Chad

McCail; Tom and Eugene McCoy; Declan McGonagle; Denise McTiernan; Fiona Melvin; Friedrich Meschede; Ute Meta Bauer; David Metcalfe; Judith Milburn; Jeremy Millar; Angela Miller; Philip Milmore; John Milner; Robert Miniaci (Robert Film Services Inc.); Elaine Mojarebi; Mondriaan Stichting; Frances Morris; Sandy Nairne; Mark Nash; Christopher Naylor; Iliayna Nedkova; Newcastle College; Frank Newton; Nexus; Jonas Nobel; Marianne Nordgren; Hans Ulrich Obrist; Simone Oetgen; June O'Malley; John O'Neill; Julian Opie; Dr Karin Orchard; Tatsumi Orimoto; Tsuyoshi Osawa; Lynne Otter; Keith Paisley; András Pálffy & Christian Jabornegg; Desmond Patrick; Jan Parkinson; Sean Parkinson; Charles Passerelli; Colin Pearson; Deanna Petherbridge; Barbara Peart; Anna Pepperall; Brenda Phelps; Clive Phillpot; Deborah Pickering; Helen Pickering; Chris Pierce; Emma Pinwill & Martyn Price (Ripe Design); Dave Pipkin; Jaume Plensa; Port of Tyne Authority; Liza May Post; David Powell; Celia Prado; Cedric Price; Martyn Price; Kath Priest; Lesley Pringle; The Progressive Players, Gateshead; Keith Purvis; James Putnam; The Quality Hotel, Newcastle; Mark Quinlan; Joe Quinn; Neil Rami; Rank Hovis Macdougal; Vanessa Rawlings-Jackson; Melanie Reed; Bruce Reid; Cait Read; Kate Rich; John Riddy; Jane Robinson; Andrew Renton; Kathleen Robson (Audi Marketing); Katherine Rooker; David Ross; Louise Ross; Lisa Rosendahl; John Rowe; Ralph Rugoff; Jim Ryan; Anthony Sargent and the staff of the Music Centre, Gateshead; David Saxon; Ankie Schellekens;

Robert Schopen; Dr Isabel Schulz; Andrew Scott; Peter Scott; Ray Scott; Carol Shaw; Laura Shepherd; Loveday Shewell; Graham Shiel; Kathy Shield; Shipley Art Gallery, Gateshead; Janine Short; Side Gallery, Newcastle; Clare Smith; Helen Smith; Ian Smith (Hillprint); Sander Snope; Phil Snow; Sneha Solanki; Frances Spalding; Dave Speedy; Julian Stallabrass; Alison Stancliffe; Peter Stark; Chris Steele; Lynn Stephenson; Matt Stokes; Paul Stone; Jacqueline Storey; Sunderland Road Library; Surtees Hotel, Newcastle; Lynne Sutton; Swallow Hotel, Gateshead; Adam Szymczyk; Chris Tait; Roger Tames; Michael Tarantino; Andrea Tarsia; Adam Taylor; Jean Taylor; Gilane Tawadros; Gillian Telford; Geoff Thomas; Marc Thomas; Neil Thomas; Jacqui Thompson; Thomson & Craighead; Muriel Thompson; Alice Thwaite; Mike Tilley; Clive Tong; Transart AB; Mark Tribe; Andy Tulip; Stuart Tulloch; Colin Turnbull; Mick Turnbull; Wendy Turnbull; Paul Usherwood; Dan Utterstrom; Eric Villeneuve; Alessandro Vincentelli; Shaffique Visram; Mel Waller; Roxy Walsh; Marijke van Warmerdam; Martin Warrener; Vic Warren-King; Jonathon Watkins; Jude Watt; Mark Waugh; Waygood Gallery, Newcastle; Martín Weber; John Webster; Suzanne Weenink; Richard Wentworth; Andrea Wheatley; Andrew Wheatley; Ian Wheeldon; Joseph White; Mike White; Val Wigham; Paul Williamson; Adam Wilson; Ednie Wilson; Captain Gary Wilson; Jane and Louise Wilson; Janet Wilson; Pitch Wilson; Sarah Wilson; Louise Wirz; Caroline Worthington; Emily Wright and Gregor Wróblewski; Aziz Zeira.

BALTIC: THE ART FACTORY

The Building of BALTIC, The Centre for Contemporary Art, Gateshead

Published in 2002 by BALTIC

BALTIC, The Centre for Contemporary Art
South Shore Road
Gateshead
NE8 3BA, UK
Tel: +44 (0) 191 478 1810
Fax: +44 (0) 191 478 1922
www.balticmill.com

ISBN 1-903655-09-9

Edited by Sarah Martin and Emma Thomas

Design and Art direction Herman Lelie

Typesetting by Stefania Bonelli
Printed by PJ Print, London

Distributed by Cornerhouse Publications Ltd.,
70, Oxford Street, Manchester, M1 5NH
e-mail: publications@cornerhouse.org
Tel: +44 (0) 161 200 1503
Fax: +44 (0) 161 200 1504

Photographic Credits:

John Riddy: Front and back cover, inside jacket, p.2, pp.6–7, pp.10–11, p.14, p.17, p.19, pp.22–23, p.25, p.26, p.31, p.48, pp.50–51, pp.54–55, p.57, p.59, p.61, p.62, p.65, pp.68–69, p.71, p.73, p.74, p.77, pp.78–79, pp.82–83, pp.84–85, p.89, p.90, p.93, p.95, p.96.

Etienne Clément: pp.37–42.

Edmund Sumner: p.188

Architectural drawings pp.4–5, pp.181–183.
© Ellis Williams Architects, London